TOOLS FOR HELPFUL SOULS

Especially for highly sensitive people who provide help either on a professional or private level

ILSE SAND

Jessica Kingsley *Publishers*
London and Philadelphia

First published by Forlaget Ammentorp, Denmark in 2014

English language edition first published in 2017
by Jessica Kingsley Publishers
73 Collier Street
London N1 9BE, UK
and
400 Market Street, Suite 400
Philadelphia, PA 19106, USA

www.jkp.com

Copyright © Ilse Sand 2017

English language edition translated by Nina Sokol.

Library of Congress Cataloging in Publication Data
A CIP catalog record for this book is available from the Library of Congress

British Library Cataloguing in Publication Data
A CIP catalogue record for this book is available from the British Library

ISBN 978 1 78592 296 1
eISBN 978 1 78450 599 8

Printed and bound in Great Britain

CONTENTS

PREFACE   7

INTRODUCTION   9

1. Fundamental Tools   19

2. Mirroring, Empathy and Taking Breaks   28

3. How Active Should a Helper Be?   41

4. Be Aware of Feelings of Shame   46

5. Focusing on Maxims   51

6. Establishing a Meeting between 'I' and 'You'   62

7. Focus on What is Happening
between the Two of You   73

8. How to Deal with Anxiety   82

9. Important Things to Know About
Highly Sensitive People   92

10. Challenges for the Highly Sensitive Helper   108

Postscript: The World Needs Helpful Souls   122

Appendix: Write a Farewell Letter   123

Thanks to...   124

Bibliography   125

Preface

This book is a practical guide in using specifically selected, simple psychotherapeutic methods in supportive dialogues, whether they take place in a kitchen, on a hiking trip, in a clinic or at a patient's bedside.

Highly sensitive people tend to get drained more quickly than do most other people when in the company of individuals who are out of balance. That is why it is particularly crucial that on the one hand they become worn down as minimally as possible but on the other hand are capable of providing the maximum assistance to the person they are helping.

If you are highly sensitive then you know what it feels like to be burdened by the 'imbalances' in your surroundings. There are two ways for you to solve the problem: you can either remove yourself from the situation or you can try to help alleviate it. The times where you choose to help, you can utilise the tools in this book to your advantage.

Most of the tools in this book can also be used with your own self-development in mind. If you ask yourself some of the questions or do some of the exercises that you'll find in this book, you will actually be optimising and strengthening your own self-development.

The book concludes with a chapter explaining why it is both very demanding and at the same time very rewarding to be a helper when you are highly sensitive and provides instructions on how you can also tend to yourself.

I have a degree in psychotherapy within various different areas. Of the many methods that I myself employ I have chosen to select a few that are easy to use.

There are some psychotherapeutic tools, which ought to be used solely by a professional psychotherapist or psychologist. But there are also others that can be used in beneficial ways outside of the psychotherapeutic sphere, as, for example, when you help clients, patients, friends or yourself. It is the latter which I will be focusing on in this book in what will be practically a cook-book style format.

The tools are geared towards optimising a helpful and supportive conversation. However, there are many other ways to help someone. I have spoken with highly sensitive people who have either invited their ageing parents to come live at home with them, or who have spent a lot of their time caring for or helping the sick, or driving people who can't get around or working as their chauffeurs. If you are the kind of person who mainly helps others with practical things and find yourself feeling over-burdened from time to time, you may benefit greatly from reading Chapter 10 in this book, which contains suggestions as to how you as a helper can better tend to yourself and your own needs.

The book is written in a language that is easily comprehensible and provides many examples so that anyone interested in psychology will benefit from reading it. It is at the same time solidly based on theories recognised within the field of psychology and on the experiences I have gained from practising psychotherapy for many years.

The many concrete examples given in the book are for the most part designed for educational purposes but contain examples of situations and statements, which I often encounter in my role as 'helper'. A few of the examples are based on real life situations and used anonymously with the permission of the client in question.

You will get more out of the book if you read the chapters consecutively, but it can also be used as a reference book.

Lading, June 2014

INTRODUCTION

For several years now I have held courses and lectures for highly sensitive people as well as met them through my practice in psychotherapy. I have heard many of them talk about how they have tried to remedy the imbalance in their surroundings or in their own lives. I have seen how much of themselves they are willing to invest in order to help alleviate it, how oppressive it gets for them when the help doesn't work and how their enthusiasm and joy blossom when they finally manage to make a positive change for others or themselves.

Many highly sensitive people report that they have tried to create a sense of peace and joy in their surroundings ever since they were children. For example, if their mother was sad they would attempt to alleviate her distress, which they might do by drawing her a picture or by behaving exceptionally well. As they grew older they were often given the role of the one whom the other members in the family would refer to if they needed help or they would be the one who would secretly help others without anyone else discovering it. However, all the others would see would be a person who seemed to get more easily tired.

A number of highly sensitive people choose caretaking as their vocation in their adult life, which is an obvious choice considering that they have practised helping others all their lives and have therefore developed excellent competences in the field. They often become popular caretakers; however, the problem for them is that they tend to become easily over-stimulated and therefore need to take more breaks than most people because if they aren't given the chance to do so they end up going home utterly exhausted, their risk of suffering adverse health effects increased due to stress.

Highly sensitive people are more impressionable. Another way of putting it is that it is easy to make an impression on someone who is sensitive. Most people like making an impression. It can be emotionally extremely satisfying to see what one has said or expressed so clearly imprinted on the faces of others.

The way in which highly sensitive people can provide a sense of relief for others became very clear to me when I was teaching a course for a small group of sensitive people. On the way to the place where the course was to be held I had almost backed into someone else's car and was trembling within by the time I reached my destination. I told the course participants about my experience and saw how my sense of shock was immediately imprinted onto all their sensitive faces. At that very moment I also felt how my own inner sense of shock disappeared; it was as though all the unpleasantness I had been feeling evaporated into thin air, leaving me with a sense of relief that increased my energy and sense of joy.

Many highly sensitive people are not at all aware of how potentially great their help can be. They typically have a desire to make the world a better place but they often do not know exactly how they should go about using their talent to do so and therefore sometimes end up wasting it by helping others with things that are not fruitful in the long run.

To unload your feelings and see them reflected in the facial expression of someone else is a great relief in the short term. But if that is all that occurs it will not necessarily lead to any kind of transformation. Or perhaps the one doing the unloading will, instead, find that he or she is dependent on the one doing the listening and so does not exercise how to contain his or her own feelings or to make the necessary changes in his or her life to get better.

Highly sensitive people who work as helpers either professionally or privately have a greater risk of being used as 'receptacles' for other people's feelings or frustrations. It is therefore very important that they find ways to look out for themselves and to help others in ways that are as efficient as possible yet without overburdening themselves.

The example below shows how you can end up becoming 'a pillow' for someone who won't take responsibility or do something about a situation, which he or she is unable to endure. The situation takes place in the private realm, but the mechanism itself, of being a passive 'receptacle' as opposed to helping the other take responsibility for his or her life, is a phenomenon which could also have taken place in a professional setting. Here is the example:

• • • • • • • • • • • • • • • • • • •

Cecilie's husband, Hans, is not thriving at his work. When he comes home to Cecilie he is usually in a bad mood. She senses how difficult it is for him to cope with and listens patiently day in and day out while at the same time feeling guilty for sometimes wishing that he wouldn't come home and disturb her with all his complaints.

The problem is that Hans won't seek the professional help he needs or won't make a decision to find another job. What makes his job just barely tolerable is the fact that he can come home to Cecilie and unload all his troubles on her. So he is using Cecilie as a pawn in his own game of avoidance. That way he doesn't have to look at his own life or make a final decision to change it.

• • • • • • • • • • • • •

Unfortunately, Cecilie's case is not unique. Whenever I supervise or give therapy to a highly sensitive person, I hear the exact same story over and over just in different versions. I think it's a shame that there are so many highly sensitive people that allow themselves to be ordered about and thereby end up becoming a part of a negative pattern instead of using their talent and skills for helping others to create more positive changes in the long run.

Highly sensitive people can clearly sense what it is that would please the one they are helping and usually feel a great urge to provide them with that particular thing. In that way they end up compensating for the others' lack of responsibility by doing things for them instead of putting their foot down so that the ones in question can learn to take responsibility for themselves, which everyone would benefit from in the long run.

It is important for the world that highly sensitive people don't end up wasting their talents but, instead, use them in the right way and in the right places.

My hope is that, through reading this book, many highly sensitive people will gain a greater awareness of their own self-worth and become better at using their competency for helping in a way that will benefit not only the world but also themselves.

Putting the book's tools to use

Most of the book's tools encourage the usage of what might be considered a very strict and controlled way of speaking with one another. However, when used outside of the field of psychotherapeutic practice, they are not intended to replace ordinary, day-to-day confidential conversations between people. Were we to always talk with one another in that way, we would end up ruining any sense of spontaneity that there may otherwise have been.

The intention of the book is that its tools may be used when ordinary conversation is no longer fruitful nor meaningful or is even counterproductive. In this kind of situation, the book's tools may be used to create a change of some sort.

The methods may be used more or less consistently. If the situation entails a conversation in a professional psychotherapeutic setting they may be used more intensely and for longer periods of time. If you are helping family or friends or are helping patients and clients professionally, the same tools may be used in a lighter version. Exactly how you choose to administer the amount or degree will depend on the situation in which you find yourself and the amount of resources the person you are trying to help has at the given moment.

Some of the tools mentioned in the book are mostly supportive in nature, as for example: listening, mirroring and giving acknowledgment or showing appreciation. These tools are accessible to everyone and applicable to all situations.

There are also tools that help to increase the speed for personal growth, as, for example, working with maxims, using the 'empty chair' technique, letter-writing assignments and focusing on everything non-verbal. There are also more seemingly innocent suggestions, such as asking the person you are trying to help to sit still for a few minutes and reflect on the connection between the two of you, an exercise which may release a whole avalanche of sorrow that has up until now been avoided as well as other repressed feelings. Consider whether the timing is right. Does the person have the energy needed to work with him or herself on a psychological level or is he or she between jobs, going through a divorce, moving or going through some other ordeal, in which case it might not be the best time for them to enhance their personal development.

Important when using the exercises

Some of the chapters contain suggestions for exercises. A good way to suggest an exercise is to start out by telling how you yourself have used that same exercise and, not least, what you have gotten out of using it, or what you have heard others who were in similar situations have gotten out of using it. No one wants to start on something new if they don't think they will be getting anything out of it in the end.

Moreover, it is important that the helper and the person being helped agree on what the end-goal is and that that end-goal is what they are going to strive toward achieving.

For example, if you want the person you are trying to help to face his or her problem and meanwhile he or she is trying to avoid the very thought of it, the communication between the two of you may become jeopardised.

In private settings, suggesting possible exercises may seem a little awkward. Whenever I myself make any suggestions in a private setting, I usually formulate it like this: 'When you talk about your dilemma at your work place, it makes me think of an exercise which I often use myself when I am facing a dilemma and am seeking more clarity. If you would like to try it I would be happy to teach you how it's done.'

If you are the kind of person who finds it too unnatural to suggest an exercise or that doing so might be crossing the line a little when helping a client, patient or a friend, you can make do with doing the exercises yourself, the goal of which is to enhance your own personal development and growth.

Practice makes perfect

Even though you have passed the theory test, it doesn't necessarily mean that you can drive a car, just like you won't learn to use the book's tools by simply reading about them. The way to become good at using the tools is through practice. I highly recommend that you start using the tools on yourself so that you become familiar with the ways in which they work.

Perhaps you can find someone you can practise with. For example, you could assemble a group that functioned as a reading group for two or more people, where you not only discuss the book you have read but also practise some of the exercises on one another. Such a group could also be a forum in which you share your experiences by using the book's tools to help alleviate the imbalances in your surroundings and where you not only practise using the exercises but take the opportunity to help one another reflect upon what exercises work best for each individual in his or her role as the helper. It can prove to be a very meaningful way to be together where you have the chance to talk about things that are important to you.

If you take yourself seriously as a helper you will automatically increase your capacity to help others also in the long run. At the same time, you are at less risk of using your talents to help others in areas where they would be better served if they learned to deal with the issue themselves. Instead, you can focus using your skills in areas where they will most likely initiate growth and strengthen a sense of joy and quality of life for others also in the long run.

When should you refer someone to a professional?

If the person seeking help is experiencing a crisis, the most important thing is to determine the extent to which there is a risk of suicide on their part. Typical signs of a crisis are: difficulty with concentration, change of sleeping habits or appetite in which the person either experiences a decrease of appetite or over-eats. I will typically start by posing questions related to these three areas if I want to determine the extent to which the person is experiencing a crisis. If it becomes apparent that that is indeed the case, I will also determine whether there is any risk of suicide. I will typically start off with a question like, 'When someone is struggling the way you clearly are right now, it is not uncommon to sometimes think that things would be so much easier if you could just end it all. Do you sometimes ever consider that?' If the person confirms that they indeed sometimes do have that thought from time to time, I continue by saying, 'Do you sometimes think about ending your life?' and the next question would then be, 'If you were to decide to end your life, how would you do it?'

It is neither dangerous nor uncommon if the person from time to time longs for death or the kind of peace associated with death. With regard to the second question, most people answer that in consideration of their loved ones they would never choose that option. If the person has considered taking his or her life, but has not considered how, then the situation is not all that urgent. However, if the person has already started collecting pills or has bought a rope, then there is reason for concern. If you fear that there is a risk of suicide, and you are not a trained psychotherapist or psychologist, the best thing is to get the person to seek professional help. However, if, for whatever reason, that does not seem to come about, I recommend that you contact a suicide prevention centre to get some help and guidance as to how you, as a loved one or helper, should approach the situation, and not least how to care for yourself under the circumstances.

If the person is experiencing a crisis he or she won't have the energy or resources to go to therapy so receiving care and support will be much more helpful than seeking professional help. If there is a risk of suicide the person will need both.

Other reasons for referrals

If the person you want to help has a serious diagnosis, for example, borderline personality disorder or schizophrenia, or has been exposed to a traumatic experience and you are not a trained psychotherapist or psychologist with a comprehensive background or under regular supervision it is better that you refer the person to a professional. However, you can support the person at the same time that he or she is undergoing a therapeutic process by listening, mirroring and acknowledging them. You can read more about mirroring and giving acknowledgment or showing appreciation in the first two chapters of the book.

There may be other situations where the best help you can give is to refer the person to someone else. If you find your task as a helper to be too burdensome, you may want to look into whether there are other helpers who are more trained in the kind of help that the person needs, and help the person to find a suitable form of treatment, if that is possible.

If you are highly sensitive and therefore more prone to being extremely affected by the situation, it is of utter importance that you are selective as to the types of people you choose to help. If, for example, you tend to get drained of energy because the person you are trying to help is very angry and tends to express his or her anger sporadically or abruptly and your sensitive nerve system has difficulty coping with it, the best thing may be to hand the task over to a more robust person who is better able to stay calm amidst an emotional uproar as opposed to a highly sensitive person who is overwhelmed and who has lost contact with him or herself.

The final thing to consider now is the type of situation where either you are the best possible helper for the person or where the person does not have the possibility to get, or the courage to seek, an alternative form of help and since you see it as crucial that he or she receives help you decide to take it upon yourself. This is where the tools come in handy.

Don't be afraid to help even though you are not a professional

Some people have such a great fear of contact that they hardly dare ask a person with anxiety what it is he or she is afraid of. Instead they choose to send the person to psychotherapy. Behind such an attitude often lies an overestimation of what psychotherapists can do and an underestimation of what ordinary people are in fact capable of.

When it comes to ordinary problems such as, for example, sorrow, fear, feelings of shame, relationship issues or other forms of problems, sometimes ordinary people are the best helpers. They have a number of advantages as opposed to a professional:

~ They can be there for a person more than one hour per week.

~ Perhaps they know the person's family and their network and can see connections that a professional, who only sees his or her client for shorter periods of time, is unable to.

~ They can offer physical consolation in the form of foot massages, soothing, touches and hugs.

~ Perhaps they love the person on a deep level and, as we know, love is the best cure there is.

~ Perhaps they have a lot of experience in life and are therefore firmly grounded, which is worth a lot more than what a newly educated young psychotherapist or psychologist can offer.

However, there may be other reasons to choose a professional. Apart from the fact that it may be necessary to try more efficient methods, the confidentiality and objectivity that professionals can provide may sometimes be an advantage.

In Chapter 1, you will find some tools that can be used both by professionals and ordinary helpers alike.

Chapter 1

FUNDAMENTAL TOOLS

Perhaps you sense that an individual in your surroundings is suffering. This concerns you, so you decide to try and help them. You may be a professional helper at work or it may be in relation to your family or to a friend. If the person in question has already talked about what it is that is troubling him or her, you can skip the next section since it deals with how you can start a conversation about the well-being of someone else.

It is best to start the conversation by saying something about yourself as opposed to starting it by asking a question. If you start with, 'How are you?' the person in question may not be sure whether you are just asking to be polite and are therefore expecting a mere 'Fine, thank you' in response, or whether you are, in fact, truly interested. Below are a few examples of how you can begin a conversation:

~ I have been wondering how you've been doing.

~ I've been worried whether you are doing okay or whether there is anything wrong.

~ I have noticed that you've been looking sad and worried lately and was wondering whether there was anything that I could help you with.

The situation in which you choose to address the person may be of significance. If you are the type of person who prefers sitting at a table across from the other person so that you can have good eye contact with them, be aware of the fact that not everyone likes to be approached that way. A lot of people prefer talking about difficult feelings while they are doing something else because otherwise it gets too intense for them. So, for some, the best situation is when they are driving a car or washing the dishes.

Once the conversation has begun, you can show your continued interest by encouraging the other person to tell you some more or by asking them questions. Some questions are better than others.

Open questions as opposed to closed questions

You can distinguish between open and closed questions. The more possible answers there are, the more open the question.

You can ask about something specific, like, 'What did you do yesterday?' 'How's it going at work?' 'How's your (aging) mother doing?' But such direct questions can sometimes be rather irritating for the one you are trying to help if he or she would rather be talking about something completely different. At worst, the person may end up feeling like he or she is being interrogated.

But by posing the question, 'Is there anything you feel like telling me?' you are allowing the person in question to choose the subject, which can then be followed by an encouragement to continue by saying, for example, 'Tell me some more about that.' After you have spoken about it for a while, you may be in doubt as to whether the person has more to tell, to which you could ask, 'Is there more you'd like to say?', which is a question that can be repeated several times.

Ask for something concrete

When we refer to things in general terms we tend to create such a distance that we become indifferent to them on a personal level. The dialogues we remember best are the ones that have touched us in some way emotionally and in order for them to do that, we need to dig down and unearth specific experiences.

If the one you are helping tells you, for example, that he or she struggles with being too impatient, it might be a good idea to ask him or her to describe the particular situations where their lack of patience tends to emerge as a problem. When we talk about our own experiences we sense the feelings that are associated with them. And the more specific we get when speaking about things, the greater the chances are that the impressions the helper gets correspond to the reality which the person in question is referring to.

Without any specific examples, the helper may imagine that the one he or she is helping has difficulties waiting for his or her turn when standing in line at the supermarket and therefore more easily gets into conflicts with the other customers. However, if the person being helped was asked to give a specific example, it would allow her to give you a more in-depth answer and she may, for example, tell you that for the past 15 years she has been waiting for her husband to change his ways, as he always promises her he will, and that she tends to generally lose her patience because of it. This would be information that would make things look entirely different.

Focus on wishes and inner resources

Many people are not aware what their deepest wishes and desires are and end up bumbling through life seemingly without any particular goal or direction. As helpers we tend to focus solely on the problems right in front of us. When encountering a problem in the mundane world we are accustomed to identifying the problem and fixing it. However, human beings are very complex and there is rarely only one reason why they don't thrive. Once we start focusing on the problems, we risk drowning in them ourselves.

It is much better to start by focusing on one's wishes., because if you don't know what the person you are trying to help wants in life you risk helping them in the wrong way.

Their wishes should dictate how you help them. There is a specific exercise, which I always ask the person I am helping to practise. I tell them the following: 'Visualise a concrete and, for you, ideal situation so that when you experience it you will feel happy and content.'

If you are highly sensitive then you are most likely good at visualising your own wishes and desires and must therefore be aware of the fact that it can be hard, or even practically impossible, for others to do the same. If the person you are helping finds it difficult to do the visualisation, you can try using your own empathic ability and imagination by suggesting, for example, some of the following situations.

Imagine:

~ that your husband tells you that he is very grateful to be married to you

~ that you sing in a choir

~ that you have an entire day to yourself from morning to night

~ that your boss tells you that you are doing a great job

~ that your mother lovingly strokes your hair

~ that you ride out into nature on your bike with camping gear

~ that your sister enquires about your current interests.

Use your imagination based on the specific situation of the person you are trying to help to work out your suggestions. If the person you are trying to help answers that he or she would feel happy and satisfied with one or more of your suggestions, then both of you will know what it is she or he is longing for.

If this exercise doesn't work and the one you are trying to help still doesn't know what it is she or he wants then the feeling of envy may be of help. If, for example, he or she thinks back on situations in which there was a sense of envy on his or her part it may be helpful in discovering what it is he or she is actually longing for.

Focusing on wishes can transform anger into sorrow

If the one you are trying to help is angry it would be beneficial if you could get them to tell not what others or the individual thinks they ought to have done, but instead what the individual wished had happened. When we focus on the wishes that never got fulfilled, we tend to get sorrowful. You can help the individual to move on by guessing, as for example: 'I understand why you are struggling right now. You probably wish that:

- ~ your ex-boyfriend had fought harder for the relationship instead of leaving you

- ~ you could have kept your job

- ~ your father was still alive

- ~ your employer had been better able to appreciate your work'

…or whatever it is the individual is angry with. If he or she responds by becoming more sorrowful than angry, you can try to get him or her to stay on track by asking how he or she wishes their life looked now.

Some of us have learned that it is bad to make others cry. But most people need to cry more than they actually ever do. So if the person you are trying to help ends up crying, then you have probably helped them a good part of the way. With anger, one risks ending up with a feeling of bitterness and hatred and if one gets caught in these emotions one will become more dead than alive in the world. But sorrow is different. Sorrow is a process and it is full of life and much easier for a sensitive helper to be around.

If the one you are helping has, after the conversation with you, become more aware of what he or she wishes for in life, then it has been a valuable experience. There may be various problems hindering him or her from reaching their goal and there is nothing wrong with also talking about those things. However, if too much time is spent focusing on problems, there is a risk that the one you are trying to help will take it too hard to be constructive and lose the energy. When that happens, it is time to shift the focus from problems to inner resources.

Ask not only about problems, but also wishes and inner resources

Here is a list of questions that focuses on the problems:

- ~ What is stopping you from feeling good?

- ~ Why haven't you already achieved the things you want?

- ~ What could be the reason why you are feeling bad?

Those questions focus on the things that are wrong. Below is a list of questions where the focus is on inner resources:

- ~ How do you go about managing?

- ~ How did you manage to get through that difficult period?

- ~ What inner resources did you have?

- ~ Have there been times in your life when you didn't have the problem?

~ When do you feel at your best? And what is it about it that makes you feel so good? And can you do more of it?

~ What is it about you that has prevented you from becoming a criminal, addict or homeless person on the street?

~ What was it about you that your grandmother liked so much?

~ Make a list of positive statements that others have said about you through the years.

~ Make a list of various challenges that you have overcome and problems that you have solved.

Some people start out by talking about the ones that have helped them when I start asking some of the above questions, whether it was a nice school teacher or a caring grandmother. They usually aren't too eager to take any credit themselves for the fact that they got through things all right. Sometimes I find myself having to ask several times before they start focusing on their own act of courage, willpower, creativity, inner resourcefulness and stamina.

An alternative to enquiring further into the problem actually entails creating a certain amount of distance to it for a little while. This is a particularly good idea if the problem is so predominant for the one you are trying to help that it overwhelms them to an extent that they tend to become agitated just talking about it. You can help them create a distance to it by asking the questions listed below:

'Imagine that it is now six months into the future. It is summer and you are walking along the beach as usual and as you are doing so how do you think you will look back upon the problem you are currently grappling with?'

Or:

> 'Imagine that you have found a solution for your problem. What
> would you then do which you normally don't do now because
> of your problem?'

The answer to the last question may consist of actual actions
– actions which the one you are helping can get started on
already now and which may help to initiate a positive change
for them.

It's not wrong to ask about problems and the one who is in
need of help often tends to take the initiative him or herself.
As a helper it is important to remember also to talk about
their inner resources, about the things that lift their energy
and mood. This is especially important if the person you are
helping is depressed or highly sensitive because then there is
a good chance that he or she has forgotten to focus on those
things on his or her own.

Summary

When you start a conversation with someone whom you
want to help, the best thing is to begin by asking them an
open-ended question so that he or she feels entirely free
to talk about the things that are most important to him
or her.

If what they say to you starts sounding very generalised
or abstract, try asking them to give you a concrete example.
That way, chances that you will both share more or less
the same mental images when talking about the subject
will increase. Moreover, it will help the person you are
listening to get closer to him or herself.

A confidential conversation can easily end up revolving
around problems. Just like a child who has scraped his
knee, many people find it difficult to focus on anything
other than the pain they are experiencing. By shifting the

focus from problems to inner resources, you soften the mood and bring some light into the darkness and it can be a particularly good way of concluding the conversation so that the person you are trying to help can hold their head high.

Taking an interest in wishes and personal resources can pave the way for developing a new and more complete image of one's self. In the following chapter I will present various ways of dealing with the things the other person tells you, whether they be in connection with problems or inner resources.

Chapter 2

Mirroring, Empathy and Taking Breaks

In this chapter I will present a way of engaging in conversation which is much more controlled than we are used to. It will become apparent that there is not much room for spontaneity and it will probably seem superficial in the beginning to have to follow the model's instructions step by step. But once you have sufficiently practised them, you will find that you can use the methods more freely and naturally than when you started.

If you are helping family or friends the model will have to be applied to a lesser degree than if you are working as, for example, a psychotherapist. In the latter case you may use the model intensely during the entire duration of the therapy session. If used outside of therapeutic practice, you should perhaps only use the model in small durations that last a few minutes at a time. Do whatever feels natural to you. With practice you will eventually discover your own style.

Limited information and silence

If you want to be thorough it is important to be slow. Just take one thing at a time. It is not a matter of accomplishing as much as possible but, rather, of going into depth with things.

Take your time and remember to take breaks or pauses. Do not allow the person you are helping to over-stimulate you with too many words because then you risk becoming a poor helper. You can, if applicable, make your own list of good sentences to say if you need to lower the pace of the conversation. Below are some examples of what I use:

~ Let's sit still together for a moment and think about what you just said.

~ It's going very fast now. Let's try to slow down the pace; that way I'll better be able to follow you. Let's start by sitting together quietly for a moment.

~ Just one moment! I just need to sit here for a little while and digest what you just told me.

~ I can hear that you have a lot you want to tell me. But it's better that we speak thoroughly about one particular topic rather than chatting away about others. So try sitting still for a little while and consider what you want to focus on.

If you find it hard to interrupt another person because you are afraid of seeming impolite it might be a good idea to ask the person about it from the start. You can for example say, 'In order for me to help you, I need to be able to interrupt you every now and then so that we can take a break. Is that okay?'

You can also bring your sense of discomfort over having to make interruptions out into the open by for example saying, 'I am sorry if you find it uncomfortable that I interrupt you every now and then, but I have to take breaks in order to be a more attentive listener.'

Sitting quietly together

I am often told in response to a conversation that the most effective part of it was the two minutes where we sat quietly together. That is why I often stop the conversation and ask for some silence. Such breaks provide more depth to the conversation and that is extremely valuable both for the recipient as well as the helper.

Perhaps you are thinking that being silent is something the person you are helping can just as well practise on his or her own and that it is really more about letting the person express themselves when they are together with you. But being silent together with someone else is completely different from being silent alone by yourself. If you sit together quietly while making eye contact every now and then, it can make a huge impact.

Highly sensitive people are perfectly capable of enjoying long breaks and actually need the peace of mind it provides so that they can better absorb their many impressions. If the person you are helping is a more active and extroverted type it may be a good idea to start off by taking very short breaks in silence since having to sit with someone without talking may make someone who is used to speaking in an endless stream very tense and uncomfortable.

If the only thing you are really doing as a helper is creating a breathing space of silence which will allow the person you are helping to take his or her time and slow down the pace, that in itself may be enough for something far more fruitful to arise for the person than what they are normally used to.

Mirroring

Mirroring is a very simple method that can make a great impact. One of the many advantages of it is that it slows down the pace which we are normally used to speaking in, allowing both the listener and the speaker to get a chance to catch up. The way you practise mirroring is by repeating what you have heard. An example of this is shown below:

Anne: Last Friday when I went over to my parents' house my father was sitting in the armchair looking tired and sad. I went over to give him a hug but it was as though he wasn't there at all.

Helper: You just told me that when you came home last Friday your father was sitting in the armchair looking tired and sad. You gave him a hug but it was as though he wasn't there at all.

Anne: Yes and then I went out into the kitchen and asked my mother whether everything was all right. She turned away from me and at first I got irritated but then I saw that she was crying.

Helper: You went out to the kitchen and asked your mother about it. She turned away from you and you got irritated but then you saw that she was crying.

Anne: Yes, and then I felt a sudden sense of tenderness toward my mother and wanted to hug her but she pulled away from me and said, 'Your father is sick and crying over it won't help. It won't help. Nothing is going to help, I just have to get through this.'

Helper: You felt a sense of tenderness toward your mother and wanted to give her a hug but she pulled away and said that your father was sick and that it wouldn't help crying and that she just had to get through it.

After mirroring you can check up on it by asking, 'Did I remember the most important things or was there something I missed?'

It may sound very simple but it is actually difficult and requires a lot of practice. The thing that usually goes wrong for most people is that the person telling his or her story manages to tell too much of it before the listener has had a chance to mirror him or her, thereby making it impossible to accurately recall exactly what was said.

As a listener you need to interrupt the flow of information, so you get it divided in sufficient small intervals, allowing you to remember and mirror fairly accurately. It is not necessary to repeat the exact same words. In fact, you can get rid of the filling words, which will make it more brief, as long as you stick to repeating the most essential words.

As a listener you may now and then want to become creative with the words you are mirroring and end up using words which you find to be just as sufficient if not more so. It is, however, very important that when mirroring you use the same words even if you think you sound like a parrot. Because every time you add another word you are inadvertently making your own interpretation and that interpretation will most likely say more about you than about the person you are listening to. By choosing to use the same words as the person telling his or her story, you allow him or her, with you as their witness, to follow their own path without getting disturbed by your ideas or evaluation.

That is why it is a good idea to practise mirroring that which the other person is saying as precisely as possible. Even if doing so for a longer period of time feels superficial. The tool is not intended to be used in its purest form for long periods of time, at any rate. But during the time you spend practising it, you might as well be as consistent as possible. Once you have sufficiently practised using it and have the method down pat, you will have the capacity to alternate between other ways of responding. Or use the tool when having ordinary conversation, as for example, when listening to something which you consider to be particularly important or when you need to slow down the pace.

Mirroring may not seem like a big deal, but it is extremely important. You repeat almost the same words, but in *your* tone and the person you are helping will search your gaze as you repeat their words to see if they make any sense to you and whether or not you think they are acceptable. If you mirror back to them a sense of respect and understanding, they will feel more comfortable with being themselves in connection with the given topic. And the more comfortable with themselves they become, the stronger they will grow, whereupon they will most likely start to find solutions to their problems on their own.

The tool is particularly good if the person you are helping has had a tendency to harp on the same thing. That may be because he or she doesn't think anyone has registered what they are saying. By mirroring their complaint, you are assuring them that *you* have registered it, something which may stop them from repeating themselves and give them more space for renewal.

Once you have practised enough you can exchange the mirror method with a shorter version in which you make do with repeating a simple word of significance or a single sentence.

If you have been mirroring for a long period of time, you can finish off with an empathic remark and thereafter suggest taking a break where the two of you can sit and chew over that which has just been said and mirrored.

Empathy

Empathy is something we practise when we try to identify with another person's feelings and tell the person how we think he or she must be feeling. We may express it by saying things like, 'It must be hard being you.' We try to imagine what it was like by making guesses. And even though we sometimes may guess wrong, most people are grateful for the attempt we make at understanding their situation and take the opportunity to tell more about themselves. The basic formulation is: 'It must be…'

Below are a few examples:

Sussie: I am planning a trip.

Helper: It must be fun.

Sussie: It'll probably be more exciting than fun, maybe a little too exciting. It makes me nervous. I'm not crazy about flying.

Or:

Hans: I'm uncertain whether my marriage is going to last.

Helper: It must be hard.

Hans: Yes (getting teary-eyed).

Just like we can practise guessing other people's feelings, we can also practise offering emotional resonance. The most important thing about empathy is not so much the words you use, but more your facial expression and tone. Your voice and your facial expression can to a much greater extent synchronise with the person's emotions or mood so that he or she can sense that you have absorbed their reality into your consciousness and are thereby participating in the feeling or mood they are experiencing. Empathy can even be expressed by a mere sympathetic sound without using words.

If Hans from the previous example were to answer, 'It's really not that bad,' there may be two reasons why he is not seemingly receptive to his helper's assessment. One is that the mirroring may say more about the person attempting to do it than it does about Hans. Another possibility is that the helper is very sensitive and has therefore detected signals deriving from an emotion, which Hans is not yet aware of or does not wish to confess.

Some people try to avoid being offered empathy because they do not want to get too close to what their own feelings are at the moment. An empathic remark may be the last straw and they risk bursting into tears. And that may not exactly be what the person wants while waiting in line at the supermarket. That is why it is important that the circumstances are suitable when you decide to approach someone with an empathic remark. Make sure that there aren't other bystanders and that you have enough time to deal with them in a compassionate way if they do suddenly burst into tears.

When you practise empathy you are showing an interest in trying to understand the person whom you are helping and that is especially important when you start your work in helpful communication because it develops a sense of security and desire to collaborate.

If empathy is too hard

Many sensitive people have a natural talent for listening with empathy but for some it is still difficult under certain circumstances. If it is difficult for you to identify with another person's feelings and to get on their wavelength it may be due to several reasons:

~ You lack practice.

~ You are not comfortable enough in the relationship you have with the person or with the situation so you are unable to sense yourself properly or to validate your own emotions.

~ You do not have experience in sensing or feeling what is being told to you.

~ You are unable to mirror another person with empathic resonance if the other person expresses feelings which you do not feel comfortable with. Perhaps what they are telling you reminds you of a bad experience you yourself have had but which you have forgotten or repressed. If these experiences have not been adequately dealt with, you will have no desire to listen to the other person.

Whatever the reason may be, rest assured that it is always something that you can work with.

Acknowledgment and comprehension

If the person you are helping has revealed something about themselves, which they have never told anyone else before, it is particularly important that they know that whatever they have said makes sense to you.

Below are some examples of how you can express acknowledgment and comprehension:

'When you tell me that you have not heard from your father for many years, I understand why it was overwhelming for you when he called. It's good that you told him that you needed to digest the surprise and that you would call back when you were ready.'

Or:

'It is difficult for me to understand exactly how you are feeling right now because I have always had a close relationship to both my parents. But your strong reaction makes sense since you haven't seen him for many years.'

The combination of various tools

The various methods described above can be combined in different ways. Once you have gained experience in using each individual tool you will have the resources needed to experiment more with combining them.

Below is an example:

Jens: My daughter is having trouble reading and her Danish teacher has now suggested that she attend a special class for children who have problems reading where the only subject the students will have for six weeks will be Danish. This worries me because it may mean that she'll fall behind in the other subjects. I'm also considering whether it might have something to do with me...

Helper: Wait a second, I just want to ensure that I've understood you. You said that your daughter has difficulty reading and that her Danish teacher has suggested that she attend a special class for six weeks. You are worried that she may fall behind in the other subjects. And you were about to tell me? (demarcation of information and mirroring)

Jens: I'm worried and upset that it may be because I haven't spent enough time helping her to learn how to read. I don't know how much time the other parents have spent helping their children and am thinking that I may not have helped her enough.

Helper: You are worried and upset that it may be because you haven't spent enough time helping her (mirroring).

Jens: Yes, because I think my daughter deserves to get the very best and I know that I don't always fit the bill.

Helper: You think your daughter deserves the best and you know that you don't always fit the bill (mirroring). That must be hard (empathy).

Jens: Yes (tears in his eyes).

Helper: I think your daughter is lucky to have a father who really worries about his daughter's well-being and thinks she deserves the best (appreciation).

Jens: (Smiling)

Helper: How about if we sit together in silence for a moment?

For most people, receiving another person's undivided attention for more than two minutes is a rare phenomenon. For some, it may feel like being washed over with love, something which can be very nourishing for the soul.

You can imagine the above sequence as being part of a long chain of mirroring sessions or you can imagine the listener suddenly saying in the middle of a normally confidential conversation, 'What you just said right now seems very significant. Let me just repeat it,' in which the above sequence of mirroring may be used, whereupon the conversation can continue as usual. The various parts of the conversation as, for example, listening, mirroring, showing empathy, acknowledgment and sitting together in silence, may be used in a different sequential order and you can choose to omit some of the answers if they don't come naturally. If the person you are helping is particularly hectic it may be a good idea to start off by sitting quietly together for a moment...perhaps an empathic remark is what is needed for the person to open up and talk about something painful.

The significance of perceiving and acknowledging another person

Telling our personal story in a setting where we are met with acceptance through emotional resonance can be most fruitful in terms of personal growth. It may be experienced as an affirmation of emotional experiences, even of a person's very existence.

Sometimes we become very focused on a specific act of change, which we think might benefit the person we are helping. It is, however, always a good idea to start by acknowledging that which already is. In order for someone to dare to change his or her situation it is important that they have their feet strongly planted on the ground. You have to know who you are and know that you are perfectly all right first and foremost in your own eyes but preferably also in someone else's. When we feel loved we have more courage to experiment and learn something new.

If you want to help another person grow stronger have to show them empathy and acknowledgment and mirror them. If you say to the person that it would be better if they, for example, were more extroverted, it will have the opposite effect; the person will feel unloved the way they are and become sad, inflexible and even more introverted. This is called the 'paradoxical law on change'. We do not change when we are under pressure; that will only make us feel insecure and when we feel insecure the worst sides of a person tend to emerge. We may then become sceptical, inflexible and unwilling to let go of our tendency to maintain control and retain old habits, self-images and many other things. As the founder of analytical psychology C.G. Jung expressed it, 'Nothing will change until you accept that which is' (Jung 1948). Søren Kierkegaard also emphasised the significance of understanding a person's immediate situation before trying to help them make a change in their lives (Kierkegaard 1998, p.45).

That is why achieving, mirroring and empathy are important and necessary fundamental tools.

When you start practising these methods you will discover that you are less attentive in the immediate situation than you were before. It is demanding to have to do something new and you will grow tired more quickly as long as you are unused to using the tools. But once you grow more familiar with them you will feel more confident when having the conversations and thus get better results.

Having structured conversations that are slow paced and in which there are breaks is especially beneficial for highly sensitive people. Not only does it help avoid over-stimulation but it also gives a person the opportunity to keep up with what is going on.

Summary

...ks is invaluable during conversation. They ... and air with them, allow for depth and the ... to sense yourself and digest the things that ... been said. We are unaccustomed to having breaks du... conversations. Oftentimes people tend to interrupt one another before anyone ever gets a chance to finish what they were saying. Or perhaps while we are listening we are thinking about what we want to say next and so each party may end up going away from the conversation with a sense of deep frustration because no one feels that they were properly heard or taken seriously. Even though it may seem superficial to take quiet breaks like these, it does give the conversation a certain quality.

Another method which ensures that the person you are listening to feels that he or she is being heard is mirroring. It is a very simple method yet it is not easy. It takes a lot of practice to become good at using it. If you invest a lot of time into getting it down pat you will be able to pull it out of your hat whenever you need a conversation to go slower or if you want to ensure that the person you are listening to feels that he or she is being heard.

Empathy is oftentimes something that is lacking in many situations because there is so much focus on efficiency. Many people long for empathy but seldom experience it. When you practise empathy the receiver is given a gift, which may provide him or her with a renewed self-perception and courage to live and be true.

Some people seem to be under the impression that the more active the helper is, the more beneficial it is for the person he or she is helping. In fact, the contrary is true: the less the helper says and does, the more efficient his or her help will become. There will be more about this in the next chapter.

Chapter 3

How Active Should a Helper Be?

Imagine a line where you at the one end have an active pole and on the other a passive one. When you are at the active pole you are focused on asking questions, suggesting possible interpretations of what you hear or giving advice. When you are at the passive pole you tend not to do much other than just be present.

Below are some dialogues. The first one is with a very active helper, the other with a very passive one.

Example with an active helper:

Orla: I just got fired from my job and in a few months I will have to put our house up for sale unless I find another job, and that's not such an easy thing when you're 56.

Helper: What can you do?

Orla: I don't know.

Helper: How about putting an ad in the newspaper?

Orla: I could, perhaps, but...

Helper: You could also create a LinkedIn profile.

Orla: True, but I'm not good with the internet.

Helper: Listen, I have an idea. You know Peter, whom we both know...

Example with a passive helper:

> Orla: I just got fired from my job and in a few months I will have to put our house up for sale unless I find another job, and that's not easy when you're 56.

> Helper: That's a real problem.

> Orla: I haven't told my wife yet.

> Helper: Oh (warm and sympathetic tone).

> Orla: I don't know how I'm going to tell her.

> Helper: No.

> Orla: I don't know what to do.

> Helper: I wish I could tell you.

> Orla: I could of course buy the newspaper and look in the job section.

> Helper: Yes.

> Orla: But first I better go home and tell Else.

> Helper: Yes.

Notice how much the passive helper is able to speak with the person eye to eye. He does not in any way attempt to be smarter or know better. In the active role we tend to position ourselves as someone looking down from a higher level, thereby implying, 'I am now going to help you with your problem.'

They are two very different ways of helping someone and neither is always right. If the person you are helping has a moderate or slight depression or is less intelligent you need to be more active as opposed to if the person you are helping is full of energy and resources and good at reflecting on things on their own.

Most people prefer to be at the active pole and so tend to be more active than is really beneficial. This applies a little bit more to men than to women. When I have couples therapy it sometimes becomes apparent that the man takes on a very active role and wants to find solutions to the problem while the woman really just wants to be listened to with empathy. However, women can also have a tendency to want to be efficient as opposed to just sitting together with the person they are helping.

Activity on the part of the helper may be due to their sense of eagerness. It may also have to do with a wish to assume a role as superior. When you are active, pose questions and give advice, you may feel very intelligent, helpful and more competent than the person you help. But too many words can easily disrupt what is happening between the helper and the one that is receiving help. Eye contact and all other non-verbal signals are far more important than words.

Highly sensitive people are generally good at being at the passive pole. According to a questionnaire study led by American researcher Elaine Aron (which she wrote about in a newsletter dated 18 March 2014), they are, for example, more willing than most to hold a dying person's hand, which is a situation where using one's skills in being active is very difficult. In that kind of situation, there is no need for clever questions or suggestions as to what can be done.

If you still sometimes become too active and impatient it may be because you have a hard time withstanding the other person's pain or because you don't feel that you are helping enough in being so passive. But it is often the contact itself, meeting someone face to face, that helps much more than clever input.

You can be passive in a way that is bad both for you and the one you are helping. If you as a helper allow yourself to be drowned by the words of the other so that your sense of presence disappears it is bad not only for the one you are helping but also for you. So there is one area where it is crucial that you are always active and that is in relation to controlling the pace of the conversation and making sure that there are breaks so that you both are able to follow what is happening, also on a deeper level.

If the person you are helping is good at reflecting it is sometimes enough just to listen and be attentively present. The person will enjoy talking and will feel included in your consciousness and thereby gain the energy needed to make the necessary changes in his or her psyche or surroundings.

To be a passive helper as in the example above may sound simple and easy. But it is not. Most people get energy from speaking and lose energy by listening for longer periods of time. Listening with empathy and helping to absorb the things which are painful is on a deeper level more demanding than being active and giving advice. If you are good at listening with empathy an important task for you is to manage your time so that you don't become exhausted.

Highly sensitive people are often more willing to hold back, sense what the other person is feeling and offer empathic resonance, all of which are invaluable in a situation in which you are helping someone. When you get tired of listening and absorbing, you can change and become more active or take a break. Don't let others abuse your talent for listening and absorbing their feelings so that you end up becoming a crutch as opposed to a constructive helper. The person you are helping also has to be willing to do what he or she can to improve their situation.

Summary

If as a helper you are able to respond to the other person's emotional resonance you can confirm the other person's emotional experience with very few words, and in some instances their entire existence, which may give them the experience of being deeply accepted and be utterly life-giving to them. Such a process can easily be disrupted if the helper is too busy coming up with clever ideas in an attempt to fix the other person's problems. However, being able to take on both a passive and an active role is most certainly a good thing.

If the person you are helping isn't very resourceful or if you as a helper are running low on energy, it can sometimes be good to be comparatively active.

It may also be the actual topics of the conversation that determine how active the helper needs to be. If feelings of shame emerge it is important to be extra slow and thorough, which is what the next chapter will deal with.

Chapter 4

BE AWARE OF FEELINGS OF SHAME

Shame comes from not being seen. It can also come from being treated badly. Most people have something or a lot about themselves or their past stories which they are ashamed about. We tend to conceal that which we are ashamed of. And that is problematic because a memory filled with shame needs to get out into the light before it can be sufficiently worked through so that it will eventually lose its power.

At this point it is a matter of proceeding with caution. If the person I am helping tells me that there is something she can't talk about I slow down the pace and acknowledge her courage in confiding to me the fact that there is something that is hard for her to share. I encourage her to take the time she needs should she at some point find it appropriate to tell me about it. At the same time I say something about knowing how painful having feelings of shame can be and that they can be treated if they come out into the light.

Some people think their secret is so shameful that it seems completely impossible for them to ever let it come out in the open. On the following page are a few examples of deep shame.

Example 1

Hanne once fell madly in love with her male boss. After having kept it to herself for several months she finally sent him an email where she told him about her feelings.

She then received a brief and clear letter of rejection from him and shortly afterward was demoted to a lower position in the company. She never told a soul. She tried to forget the episode but when it surfaces every now and then she shrinks with such shame at the mere thought that it makes her wish she could disappear from the face of the earth.

• • • • • • • • • • •

Example 2

• • • • • • • • • • • • • • • • • •

Every time Jens has to go to a social event he carries a small hip-flask in his pocket. He takes a swig just before the event starts. That way he can better deal with the social challenges. He has used alcohol in that way ever since he was a teenager. No one knows about it, not even his wife to whom he has been married for 12 years. It is so shameful to him that he can't ever imagine telling anyone about it.

• • • • • • • • • • • •

When a shameful feeling is about to surface into the open, it is important that it doesn't happen too fast.

If it is apparent that the person is feeling deep shame, I sometimes suggest taking a more gradual approach to disclosing it. For example, in Jens' case I would suggest the following:

~ That he write a letter about it to a deceased grandmother or another loved one with whom he felt safe.

~ That he tell it to someone he is not afraid of losing, as for example, a psychotherapist, a doctor, a distant acquaintance or counsellor on the internet whom he can contact anonymously.

~ That he write it in a letter to an important person, without sending it.

~ That he tell a part of the story in the past tense to an important loved one, for example, to a spouse. Jens could for example say, 'When I was 18 I would always take a swig from a hip-flask before attending a social event,' whereupon he may build up the courage to add, 'and I have been doing the same thing ever since.' However, he may not be ready to add the last sentence until after months have passed.

Shame can be a very strong feeling as in the examples above. But oftentimes we encounter it in milder versions and in such instances we often refer to it as a feeling of embarrassment. When a shameful feeling is mild or moderate, revealing it gradually is usually not necessary.

It may not be something negative that one is ashamed about. Some people are ashamed of the love they felt for someone if it was never recognised or remained unrequited. It does not have to be anything dramatic or forceful. Some people feel ashamed over things that others would consider to be mere trivialities. For example, you might feel ashamed over the fact that you tend to blush, get easily teary-eyed, forgot to flush the toilet once, or over the fact that you do not have a sun-roof on your car.

Whether there is talk of an all-encompassing form of shame or sense of embarrassment, the cure is the same. The sense of shame is healed if it is brought out into the open in relation to another person who sees it and acknowledges it for what it is. It is important that the person feeling the shame gets a sense that the listener can withstand hearing about it and is able to maintain a connection with the speaker without judging him or her or becoming distant.

When another person confides their shame to us, it is important to remain a passive helper (see Chapter 3). The connection here is so important that it must not be disturbed by too much activity or too many words on the part of the helper. A helper who is too active might, for example, in his eagerness to help, come out with the following rather unfortunate remark, 'That's nothing to be ashamed of.' Though it may be well-meaning, the person feeling the shame will only end up feeling even worse about themselves than before. What the person really needs is first and foremost to know that he or she is being heard and that the connection between them and the helper remains intact.

Sofie: I think it is so shameful that I don't have a job.

Helper: Yes.

Or:

Jens: My need to carry a hip-flask shames me.

Helper: Yes.

Avoid saying anything more in the first instance. The break that will be coming up shortly will be important. Let him mirror himself in your gaze, that is, if he is at all prepared to even look up. Otherwise, give him some time. Then you can start expressing a little empathy by saying something like, 'It must have been very lonely carrying that secret for all those years.' Or tell him that he is not the only one in the world who has felt shameful about something by saying something like, 'I know what it means to feel ashamed about something. I also have had my share of it.'

There is a need for people who are able to face shame no matter where they go. On the face of it, the method sounds very simple. You just say yes and maintain a sense of connection with the person you are helping. But it is not as straightforward as it may sound. As a helper you need to have the ability to accept your own feelings and be able to maintain a connection with another person who is going through something very painful. In my experience, people who have both feet firmly planted on the ground and who have a healthy view of themselves can be just as good at dealing with people in their shame as any professional.

Summary

Shame is a very painful and lonely experience. It may make a person feel like they want to disappear from the face of the earth or become invisible. To do the opposite, to talk about your shame, can make a person feel very anxious. At the same time it is also the way to move forward and become more alive and visible to the world. There lies a great potential for growth by working through one's sense of shame. Having an experience of authentic emotional contact with another person regarding a shameful feeling can actually be ground-breaking.

When working with shame it is important to be slow, cautious and comparatively passive (see Chapter 3).

If you listen to another person's story concerning his or her feeling of shame you have most likely helped him or her to set themselves free, allowing them to expand their own self-image and the possibility to take action in their lives.

Empathy and a strong connection can sometimes increase the energy and sense of joy in the person you are helping so that the problems may start to naturally solve themselves. At other times there may be a need to initiate a development process in areas where the person seems less aware of themselves. In the following chapter I will present an area of focus that often optimizes the developmental process.

Some people continue to get stuck in the same problems and have difficulty moving on no matter how much of a strong connection or sense of empathy is offered to them. It could be due to the fact that the possibilities they have to take action are somehow limited because of counterproductive maxims.

Chapter 5

Focusing on Maxims

Aside from the laws and rules that society delegates, all people have a certain set of rules or maxims, which they have either inherited from their parents or created themselves and which they follow. Most people are not fully aware of their own maxims and may benefit from focusing on them.

Below are some examples of maxims:

~ I must never make mistakes.

~ I must never be conceited.

~ I have to be outstanding at everything I do.

~ I must not show vulnerability.

~ I must be exactly as others expect me to be.

~ I must be cool.

~ I must not do anything that contributes to the earth's pollution.

~ I must not overuse the earth's resources and must constantly ask myself, 'How little can I make do with?'

~ I must make sure that everyone around me is doing well.

~ I cannot have any expectations of others.

~ I must always eat healthily.

~ I must never, under any circumstances, lie.

~ I must never be a burden to anyone.

~ I must be careful not to hold myself up as better than anyone else.

~ The needs of others are more important than my own.

~ I must always be on guard and keep an eye out for anyone who might try to take advantage of me.

~ If others are angry with me it is my responsibility to make sure that they get to like me again.

~ I have to be hospitable and always happy whenever anyone knocks on my door.

~ I have to always be available for my friends should they be in need.

Maxims were created for a good purpose. Their function is to regulate our behaviours in a way that will help us do well in life. They may function as inner guide posts that help us to find the good things in life. By focusing on your maxims, you may become more aware of the fact that you are following one or several rules that end up having the opposite effect. So they either hinder you from taking proper care of yourself or allow you to continue behaving a certain way that in reality makes life more difficult and robs you of your energy without doing anyone any good in the long run. If that is the case, once you become aware of it you will be more motivated to stop it from continuing.

Many people follow rules that they themselves are not aware of. They may have inherited their parent's rules. They may be following rules, which they may have forgotten they themselves once created. It is like eating with a spoon; it can be difficult if you have never tried it before. At first you have to figure how much you should put on the spoon, how you can avoid spilling its contents and how you direct it into your mouth. Once we have learned to do it we don't give it a second thought. It happens automatically and we no longer remember how or why we are doing it in the particular way that we do.

Sometimes we follow rules we invented when we were children but which merely drain us of energy today without our realising it. Or perhaps we follow rules that derive from a completely different time. Below is an example.

· · · · · · · · · · · · · · · · · · · ·

Inga loved playing cards. For her it was a fun game, which she enjoyed. She felt slightly guilty about enjoying it so much and she didn't know why. And if there was money involved in the game, she felt she had to say flat out no.

When we started focusing on what rules were involved with games, Inga became aware of the fact that she often had heard her mother speak in a very judgmental tone about people who spend their time playing cards. Inga's mother was still alive so Inga was able to ask her mother why she thought playing cards was wrong. Inga's mother told her that her great-grandfather had once lost all the family's money playing cards.

Once Inga became aware of her own maxims regarding card games she got rid of them. A new world now opened itself to her. She became a member of two more card-playing clubs which she had always wanted to be but which hadn't been a possibility for her previously because they played for money. She was now able to nurture her passion for card games five times a month instead of just two.

· · · · · · · · · · · · ·

The more rules there are, and the more strict, the less possibility there is to take action

Imagine a map of Denmark and pretend that it is filled with all the possible ways a person can take action in life. For each limiting maxim a person has, you can cut a part of the map away.

One example might be a person whose maxim requires that she always look good so she can never just decide to stay in her nightgown for a whole day and not care about her appearance. If you have a maxim that says you must not disappoint your mother who has great ambitions for you in life, then you cannot just choose to become a chimney sweep even though that may be what would suit you best. Maxims and prohibitions eat away at a person's possibility to take action in life. Some people have so many maxims that are so strict that the 'range' in which they can take action, a range which could have been as big as the entire map of Denmark, is equivalent to the size of a small island, requiring a great imagination and a lot of energy to get something out of life when the possibilities to actually take action are so few.

The discovery of counterproductive maxims

It is particularly in situations where we have to make decisions that the maxims become more apparent to us. Questions like 'Why don't you just do what you feel like?' or 'Why don't you just stop doing the thing you don't feel like doing?' will reveal not only maxims but also values.

If the person you are helping does not reach his or her goals in life or is living an unfulfilling life it may due to unsuitable maxims. A question like 'Why don't you just...' may sound not only stupid but also irritating because of course the person has his or her reasons for acting the way they do. But the question is nevertheless important and as a helper it may be worth bearing in mind that stupid or irritating questions are sometimes the ones that make the most difference. However, it is possible to conceal the question in a polite phrase. I do that myself, especially if I am helping someone in a private setting. I may phrase the question something like this: 'When you tell me that you didn't at all want to go to your cousin's birthday, I can't help wondering why you didn't decline the invitation in the first place. I hope I am not being too bold here.'

The answer to the question is often a maxim. I mirror it by saying, 'It sounds like you have a maxim that prohibits you from allowing your need for a quiet weekend to be a priority as opposed to what your mother expects of you.' You can stop here. Once a maxim is revealed the person will become more aware of his or her reasons for acting the way he or she does and that will open up new possibilities for them. Perhaps the person will then be curious to know how a maxim can be changed. Or perhaps they won't.

If the person you are listening to expresses dissatisfaction with being limited by his or her maxim tell them that you yourself have gotten a lot out of focusing on and working through your own maxims and offer to tell them more about how they can do the same.

Below is an example of how you can work through a maxim.

Jane secretly wishes she could celebrate Christmas at a seaside resort in southern Europe. When I ask her why she doesn't seriously do something about that wish, she reveals the following maxims and values to me:

~ You have to be with your ageing parents during Christmas.

~ You cannot be egocentric.

~ It is not all right to spend so much money solely on one's self.

Once the maxims have come out in the open the natural thing to do is to take a good look at each one. Is it a good and constructive rule or does it limit you for no reason?

Working through maxims and formulating new alternatives

If the person you are helping likes to write, you can ask her to make a list of the advantages and disadvantages in connection with each maxim on two separate pieces of paper.

Jane ended up keeping her maxims but just revising them a little, which made the beach vacation a possibility. Here is what her maxims look like in their revised version:

~ You should be there for your ageing parents, but not all the time.

~ If you spend the first Sunday of Advent with them it is all right for them then to be alone during Christmas.

~ It is alright to be a little egoistic every once in a while and spend some money on one's self. In fact, in the long run it will most probably be the best for everyone that you do, because you will return home in a much better mood and feeling rejuvenated.

It can really pay off to make an extra effort to not only run those new thoughts in your mind but also to write them down on a piece of paper so that you can remind yourself of them by reading them over and over. If you don't like to write you can say the alternative rule out loud to yourself several times. It will work best, however, if you say it aloud in front of someone. If you don't want to involve anyone in your work you can say it to an old tree in the forest or to your reflection in the mirror.

As you develop new maxims for yourself you will have to undo the old ones. The best way to do that is to simply break them. The more times you break the old rules the less power they will have over you.

Undoing counterproductive maxims

Maxims are deeply connected to certain assumptions that we have about the world. If the person you are helping is having a hard time breaking a counterproductive maxim or rule it might be a good idea to examine the assumption that he or she tends to associate with it. One way of finding out what that assumption is is by asking:

~ Why do you have to…?

~ What would happen if you didn't do that?

~ Why can't you…?

When asked why she wouldn't allow herself to be egocentric, Jane answered with a response which she later realised was a verbatim repetition of what her father used to say, which was the following, 'If everyone just did whatever they felt like doing, where would that leave us?' This was a sentence which she had heard her father say on numerous occasions, as for example the time when she wanted to participate in a badminton game instead of babysitting her little brother. Looking back on the situation as an adult, she was able to see that if her father had been just a tad better at thinking creatively they could have found a different solution to the problem by either letting their grandmother watch her little brother or letting her take him with her to the badminton game where he could sit and watch her play. She decided once and for all that she would no longer allow herself to be influenced by her father's unimaginative reply which he had used back then to prohibit her from doing what she really wanted to without there being any real reason for not letting her.

When asked why she felt she ought to be there for her ageing parents during Christmas, she answered that they had been there for her when she was little and helpless and now that they were the ones who needed help, she wanted to repay them. But when she also remembered how they used to do many things that *they* felt like doing when she was little, even if it meant that she had to be babysat by others, something which she didn't always like, she changed her maxim so that she wouldn't *always* have to be there for them, and that included Christmas.

Breaking counterproductive maxims

When you dare to do something differently, or cease to do something you have always done for many years, maybe for your whole life, it is often associated with fear or discomfort.

When Jane had decided to tell her parents that she was going to a seaside resort for Christmas, she lost a couple of nights' sleep over it. The first year she was away for Christmas she was extremely concerned and worried that they were going to get sick while she was gone.

But when nothing bad happened while she was away and it turned out that the beach vacation was actually really very good for her, it became a lot easier for her the next time she was in a similar situation where she had to tell her parents that she preferred prioritising her own needs.

Some people feel the need to limit their field of action once they have become more aware of it. Perhaps they don't feel all that good about the way they behave in the world and start wanting to show more consideration for others. What happens in most cases, however, is that once people become aware of their maxims, they oftentimes want to rid themselves of some of them or just revise them a little, giving him or her the possibility to expand their field of action, as Jane did. She now had many more possibilities to choose from. All the things which she had prohibited herself from doing because she though they were too egocentric she was now reconsidering, giving her the possibility to incorporate more joyful activities into her life.

To live according to a newly incorporated maxim takes a lot of energy in the beginning. If you get pressured, scared or just tired, you will easily fall back into using the old maxims, which you most probably lived in accordance with your whole life. That is due to the fact that it takes a lot less energy to follow the old rules that come automatically to you as opposed to pulling yourself together to do something which you aren't used to doing. However, there is no reason to despair over such relapses. It is totally normal to have them and they will lessen over time as long as you insist on holding on to your new goals and remind yourself of them whenever a new situation arises.

You can recommend to the person you are helping that he or she hang the new rule up on their mirror or another place where he or she will see it often, or to tell a friend about it and ask that friend to remind them of the new rule.

Strict maxims and low self-esteem

If you have maxims for yourself that involve having to behave better than most other people, for example by being more helpful and diligent in fulfilling the expectations of others, it is often due to low self-esteem. When I asked Jane why she thought she had to always be helpful and never be a burden to others she herself was surprised by her own answer. Due to her low self-esteem, she was simply afraid that no one would want to have anything to do with her otherwise.

Strict maxims often serve the function of compensating for the fact that you do not feel good about yourself. For example, by behaving in a very friendly way a person may subconsciously hope that no one will discover just how little they are worth. If you break your maxim and discover that other people continue to like you or that they like you even more and actually find you more interesting than the way you were before, it will improve your self-esteem.

If you modify your maxims in such a way that it becomes easier for you to be yourself it will also have a positive effect on how you perceive yourself. If, for example, you allow yourself to decline a birthday party invitation because you don't feel like attending it and instead spend the money you saved by not going on a big bouquet of flowers for yourself, you are sending a signal to your own inner system that you are significant and that your needs are important.

Values

However, it is not always the case that the more we modify and ease our maxims, the better. Some maxims make a lot of sense for us to have because they are deeply anchored in certain individual values we may have. To know our values and to choose to follow them can help us to better come into our own as the unique individuals we are. Examples of values may be:

~ It is bad to contribute to pollution.

~ You have to show children extra consideration.

~ You have to be honest.

~ You cannot seek advantages at the expense of others.

Values which mean a lot to you should, of course, not be changed or worked through, but it is good to be aware of them. If you know what your principles are then you will better be able to understand why you tend to become upset in specific situations.

Summary

If the person you are helping has a hard time removing him or herself from the area in which they have problems it may be because he or she is limited by too many strict rules or constraints. Working with becoming more aware of your maxims can open up new possibilities in terms of taking more action in your life. However, a person's maxims are often deeply connected with his or her entire world view and deeper-lying convictions that will not necessarily just change from one day to the next. But if the person you are helping has started to get a sense of how he or she can better take action in his or her life by re-evaluating their maxims, then he or she is definitely on the right track.

Taking a closer look at maxims is a way to speed up the process of personal development. In the following chapter I will present certain tools that may prove to be even more efficient.

Chapter 6

ESTABLISHING A MEETING BETWEEN 'I' AND 'YOU'

Sometimes we have to get to the very heart of the pain we are dealing with before it can be changed. A lot of people spend most of their lives merely touching upon it instead of getting really close to what it is they are feeling that, on the surface, may seem frightening, but on closer inspection may be set free or, at a later point, may show them a new way to deal with an issue.

Below are a number of exercises and methods you can use to help get yourself and others closer to what matters most to you or to them in life. In the final part of the chapter I will show you a lighter version of the exercises.

From telling *about* a person to talking directly *to* them

We can spend a lot of time talking 'about' a problem. We typically have many explanations as to why we have difficulties in our lives, explanations which we will gladly share with those who are willing to listen. They may consist of stories that are both numerous and long, the purpose of which is to free us from at least parts of, if not the entire, responsibility and blame.

If you are listening to someone's story and sense that you are getting bored, the person telling the story is most probably experiencing the same thing. He or she has probably told the story before to others, perhaps even several times.

To tell 'about' someone creates a distance as opposed to talking from an 'I' to a receiving 'you'. If you can get the person you are helping to express his or her pain directly to the other party involved he or she will be able to sense their own feelings and the significance of the other person in question more intensely which may, eventually, help to clarify the situation.

You can establish a meeting between 'I' and 'you' in several different ways. One of them involves using an empty chair. You place the chair before the person you are helping and ask him or her to imagine that one of the people involved in the problem is sitting on the chair. An example might be the following: Helle had for a long time been speaking negatively about her father. I asked her to imagine that her father was sitting on the chair across from her. I could also have asked her to write a letter to him. The important thing is that she no longer refers to him in the third person 'he' but in the second person 'you'.

In other words, she won't say, '...and then he always forgets my birthday, it's as though I am no longer important to him any more.' Instead she will be saying, 'Dad, you forgot my birthday again and I'm afraid that I'm no longer important to you.' There is another example below.

. . . .

Bente explains how unfulfilling her marriage is and has plenty of stories to tell about what her husband does and doesn't do. She speaks hectically, as though she wants to say everything all at once before I will grow tired of listening to her.

I place a chair in front of her and ask her to imagine that her husband is sitting on the chair. Then I ask her to say some of things she just said to me directly to her husband. This affects her and she starts fumbling for words. At the same time I stop being bored. The fact that she is groping for words means that she is trying to formulate something she hasn't said before and I sense that the work she is now doing is fruitful.

· · · · · · · · · · · · ·

The chair method is also suitable in terms of personal development. I myself sometimes use chairs when I need to find out where I stand in terms of a difficult relationship. You can use the method without there necessarily having to be a helper present.

Using the 'empty chair' technique

Below I will provide more detailed and concrete instructions as to how to use an empty chair to get a more direct form of conversation going. I will do that based on the following example.

· · · · · · · · · · · · · · · · · · ·

Anne had a traumatic experience with her uncle Henrik. She does not wish to have any contact with him today but cannot avoid running into him during family events, and every time that happens it is problematic for her.

I place an empty chair before her and ask her to sense how far the distance should be between her chair and her uncle's. Once the chair is standing at the right distance for Anne I ask her to take a few deep breaths and sense how the chair she is sitting on is actually carrying her. Then I ask her to look over at the other chair and imagine that her uncle is sitting on it. I ask her to imagine it as clearly as she possibly can. What is he wearing? What is his posture like, his facial expression? Then I ask her how it makes her feel to have him sitting across from her. If she gets afraid I suggest we move his chair further away from hers or that she imagine him being half the size he is now or even smaller. Her task is now to formulate what she is feeling directly to him. She could, for example, say, 'Sitting here across from you makes me think of the times you would tickle me until I couldn't breathe and it makes me mad. That wasn't OK. I wasn't just a toy. I got scared of you.'

The exercise can end with Anne saying everything to him that she needs to say. She can also continue and go over and sit down on her uncle's chair where she can imagine that she is him. I will then ask her to say aloud, 'I am Uncle Henrik, I am 67 years old, sitting here in my worn shirt and looking at my niece, Anne.' She needs to try to feel what it was like to be Uncle Henrik. I talk to her as though she were Henrik and ask her, 'What is it like listening to your niece, Henrik? How does that make you feel? Is there something you would like to say to her?' He may then say, 'I didn't realise I had crossed the line until you ran away hiccuping and wouldn't play with me afterwards. I am sorry for not paying more attention to what I was doing.' He may also say, 'I don't recall that happening.'

Once the uncle is through, Anne can sit down in her own chair, whereupon she should say aloud, 'I am now Anne, I am 37 years old and sitting here looking at my uncle.' She should sense within herself whether Henrik's facial expression affects her in any way and whether there is more she wants to say. The dialogue can continue and can change from one chair to another, as long as it makes sense. It is important that the last remark that is made comes from Anne's own chair.

* * * * * * * * * * * *

I could also have asked Anne to merely visualise that her uncle is standing before her, or I could have asked her to write a letter to him and read it aloud to me next time we meet.

A letter addressed directly to the party involved has the same effect as the chair method in that it shifts the discussion from being 'about' the other person to being a direct approach on the part of an 'I' to a receiving 'you'. Suggesting the writing of a letter may also be suitable in connection with many other situations outside of the therapeutic sphere. I sometimes suggest it to friends and acquaintances and use it also to a great degree when I myself need to gain more clarity over a situation in my life.

Letter writing

Expressing the things which are troubling you has in itself a beneficial effect on your immune system. Studies show that repressed feelings may cause inner stress and stress decreases the efficiency of the immune system. It is therefore, under all circumstances, a good idea to express one's self, even if it doesn't make it further than to a piece of paper. Furthermore, when writing a letter, there is the advantage that it allows you to address the issue at hand directly to the person you are having problems with, which, in turn, gives you better access to your own feelings in regard to the relationship and the role which the other party plays for you.

It is important that the letter is directed to the person right from the start, as in, 'Dear (or Hi) Henrik.' The letter should be written as a farewell note because having a sense that something is about to be finalised tends to increase your focus and enhance your feelings. The person writing the letter could, for example, pretend that he or she will be moving halfway around the world and therefore not know whether or not he or she will ever see the person whom the letter is addressed to again. Toward the end of my book, *The Emotional Compass: How to Think Better about Your Feelings* (2016a), you will find examples of farewell letters.

Letter-writing exercises may also be used to examine your own wishes. If you write a letter from someone else to yourself that contains everything you long to hear from the person, it can sometimes be an eye-opener. Were Anne to write such a letter from her uncle to herself, my guess is that it would sound something like this:

Dear Anne,

I am terribly sorry for what I did. I did not respect your boundaries. It was wrong of me and I am ashamed of what happened. Can you forgive me?

Best,

Uncle Henrik

If Anne is then able to feel that were she to receive an unreserved apology from Henrik she would be able to tolerate having contact with him again, then that means that we have been given an important piece of information as to how that relationship might be re-established.

When you write a wish-letter to yourself on behalf of someone else, the letter need not in any way be realistic. It is just a matter of allowing your imagination to run wild and let the other person say exactly what you wish they would say no matter whether or not the person would ever be able to get themselves to say those words in reality. When the person you are helping has written the letter you can offer to read it aloud. Such a letter can sometimes provide you with a sense of 'release' even though you have written it yourself. And it can help you to better understand exactly what it is you long for.

People who find themselves stuck in feelings of anger may particularly benefit by writing a wish-letter to themselves from the person they are angry at. If the person you are helping discovers what it is he or she wishes to get but can't receive, he or she can either accelerate the speed of his or her struggle to acquire it or give up on the wish and allow the anger to transform into sorrow.

Before I ever give anyone the letter-writing exercise to do at home, I always check to make sure that the assignment has been properly understood by the person and that he or she is able to complete it. I do that by asking the person to try to formulate and say aloud the first two lines and sometimes also the last line of the letter as I listen to them.

Sometimes it is hard for the person to get started. In such instances I will from to time suggest an opening line. My suggestion often begins with, 'Dear..., Thank you for...' At the back of this book I have printed a number of questions that can be used as inspiration for the person writing the letter.

In order for the letter writing to be as effective as possible, it must be read aloud to a person functioning as a witness. It may be to a therapist or a friend, as long as it is not the person to whom it is addressed.

It happens on occasion that the person who wrote the letter decides to give the letter to the person to whom it was addressed. This can sometimes be a good idea, at other times not.

Saying something to the person with whom there is a problem

Practising expressing your pain as an 'I' to a 'you' on the receiving end is always a good idea. Interfacing with the other person in real life is also sometimes a good idea, although it may have unfortunate consequences. We are often quick to brush off somebody's lament by suggesting that they say it directly to the other person's face. That may be an appropriate remark if the person who is confiding in us uses the lament as a way to get rid of her own anger and is not truly interested in knowing how she herself can get better at dealing with the situation.

But if the person confiding in us about a third party is sensitive and the person she is complaining about tends to be aggressive in their words or actions, it can seem rather harsh to reject her by telling her that she needs to say it to the person directly. If she had dared to say it at all, she would already have done so and when she instead chooses to say it to someone else it is to get help to find the courage to go through with it or help to find the right words.

Writing a letter or saying it to an imaginary person sitting on an empty chair are ways to practise finding the right words or finding the courage for a direct confrontation if that is at all advisable, which it normally isn't if, for example, the third party tends to react extremely negatively to anything that might be interpreted as criticism.

Talking directly is also something that a person can do to him or herself and it can be just as efficient. Read more about this in the following section.

Having dialogues from empty chairs when inner dilemmas must come out into the light

Empty chairs are a good tool when trying to initiate dialogues, including the ones we have more or less consciously with ourselves. Below is an example of how this can be done.

· · · · · · · · · · · · · · · · · · ·

On the one hand Hanne would like to move to the city and on the other she would rather not, and she finds that she is getting angry with herself over the fact that she cannot make a decision. I ask her to place two chairs across from one another. On the one chair sits the Hanne that wants to move into the city. On the other sits the Hanne that is very worried about the idea and that doesn't feel up to moving anywhere at all.

On the first chair I ask her to identify herself with the Hanne who wants to move and to let it reflect in her mimicry and body language. It is important that she allows herself to fully give in to talking with enthusiasm about all the pleasant things associated with living in a town. When she is completely done and has nothing more to say about it, she should move over to the other chair and let the 'concerned' Hanne express herself through body language and mimicry and express everything she is afraid of. It is also possible for her to change several times between chairs, moving back and forth between them and allowing the dialogue to take shape. It could, for example, be in the form of questions and answers. The enthusiastic Hanne might ask the worried Hanne, 'What are you so afraid of?' and the worried Hanne might ask the enthusiastic Hanne, 'What will you do if you discover that the neighbours are too loud in the new place?'

It is possible to also include empty chairs when you yourself are struggling with a personal problem or relationship where you aren't sure how to deal with it. Instead of letting it all play out inside your mind it can be a relief and also a help to clarify things by expressing them outwardly. I myself use chairs when I feel indecisive about something. On the one chair I support a specific aspect 100 per cent and on the other I argue for the opposite. At times I will have to use several chairs in order to include all the various nuances of an issue.

When you have helped draw someone's attention to their inner dialogue it is not always necessarily a given that they will end up gaining clarity. She or he may have become even more confused. But in the course of the days to come new thoughts will probably start to surface, which will help him or her to make a decision.

If a person has a tendency to become slightly confused during a conversation it may be a good sign. You may have managed to disrupt a certain pattern so that she is unable to use it in the same way as before.

Breaking old patterns

We may have the impression that if we reach a certain sense of clarity after a conversation then all is good. But sometimes things just can't move that fast. It may be necessary for you to go through a period in life where there is a lot of confusion before you are ready to get a completely new impression of yourself and the world. To go from what feels like a safe and familiar way of thinking to feeling confused and insecure about everyone and everything may be a sign that things are starting to really progress for you on a deeper level.

If you experience that the person you are trying to help actually feels worse after talking to you, it is not necessarily something you need to feel guilty about. You may have helped the person take a step further in their journey. Some people feel guilty if the person they are trying to help starts to cry. But it may be a sign that the person has really just gotten closer to him or herself.

We always feel the safest with the things that we are most familiar with. That is one of the reasons why we tend to remain stuck in old negative patterns long after our intellects have realised that those patterns no longer serve us. Venturing forth onto new paths will always be associated with a certain degree of anxiety and confusion.

Using the tools in a lighter version

If the conversation takes place during therapy, using the empty chairs and suggesting exercises that can be done at home would be obvious things to do. However, if the conversation takes place in a different setting it may feel more natural to use the same tools but to a lesser degree, that is, in a lighter version. Instead of asking the person you are speaking with to write a letter you can talk about how much you or others have gotten out of using that particular tool and ask if he or she would like to learn more about how to use it themselves.

Instead of getting a chair you can make do with asking, 'If you were to say the exact same thing that you are telling me now to the person in question, how would you formulate it?'

Summary

Much of a person's life is wasted in attempting to explain and tell stories, stories that may end up developing lives of their own and that reconfirm the self-perception which the person telling them has of him or herself. Furthermore, the stories may be really outdated in which case they should be replaced by narrations that are more up to date.

When you ask the person you are helping to tell you what is wrong using direct speech, something new and different tends to occur. It is difficult to maintain, even if it is only in your imagination, a villain-like image of a person whom you will be meeting face to face. On the contrary, in fact, in such an instance your feelings and the significant role the other plays for you will become more apparent and enhanced. The problems and stories you are used to telling about the problem will disintegrate and a new image with an accompanying new self-perception may emerge.

In the following chapter I will present yet another efficient tool that can help bring the person you are helping closer to him or herself and achieve a deeper connection with you.

Chapter 7

FOCUS ON WHAT IS HAPPENING BETWEEN THE TWO OF YOU

During a conversation, we are often so focused on the content of the words being said that we tend to overlook what is even more important, namely: the body's reaction, the mood between the two people speaking, the intention with the words and their effect. Once we start talking with each other about our way of speaking to one another and about the things that happen between us when we do, we often get much closer to not only ourselves but also to one each other.

To focus on meta-communication is an important part of psychotherapeutic practice. Outside of the therapeutic sphere the tool can be used to a lesser degree. How one can go about doing that will be explained at the end of the chapter.

In the paragraph below are a number of suggestions with accompanying questions, which you can use to help focus on the things that lie just below the surface of words.

Calculations of considerations

Before, during and after we say something most of us take various things into consideration. These considerations often say more about us and our way of being in the world than do the words we actually use. The following questions can help to focus in on these considerations:

~ What are you hoping that I will answer to that question?

~ What are you considering right now as you tell me this?

~ What would you like to get out of telling me this? For example, would you like me to come up with a suggestion or do you just need to get it off your chest?

~ What compelled you to tell me this? What were you considering before you decided to tell me this?

~ What kind of an impression do you hope I will get of you?

~ Are there ways in which you would prefer not to be seen or perceived?

~ Are you doing anything to avoid that I get a certain kind of impression of you?

But bear in mind that not everyone thinks before speaking. Some very extroverted people just say whatever comes to mind without considering, for example, whether or not the listener will find what they are saying interesting. If the person you are helping has difficulty answering the questions in this category, it may be because those questions hit too close to home or because he or she is a very spontaneous and impulsive type of person who tends not to think before speaking.

Feelings and moods

As we speak together we experience various feelings and moods. That which we express can be associated with fear, anger relief, joy, etc. That which we hear can also initiate various feelings and moods. When we start talking about the emotional reality that is moving as we communicate, an entirely new dimensions may enter the conversation:

~ What is your impression of the mood between us?

~ How do you feel right now as you tell me this?

~ My sense is that which you are telling me right now is something you have told others many times before, am I right?

~ That which you are experiencing right now as you tell me about…does it make you get any closer to your own feelings, or further away?

To like or not to like

It is often the case when it comes to communication that some of what we say or hear are things we feel good about, while there are other things which we don't like:

~ What do you think about the fact that I sometimes interrupt you and repeat some of what you have just said?

~ How do you feel about me seeing you sad like this?

~ How do you feel about the distance that there is between us? Would you like for us to move closer or further apart?

~ What do you think of the question I just asked you? Do you have a better suggestion?

~ It seems to me like you would prefer not to answer my questions. Is that true?

Questions which turn the focus toward that which we don't normally express in words can initiate entirely new forms of conversation. Here is an example of one.

· · · · · · · · · · · · · · · · · ·

Marie, who is a woman of many words, talks about her
children's friends. I am getting bored and ask, 'Why are you
talking about your children's friends?' For a moment she
is at a loss for words and then finally says, 'I actually don't
know either.' There is a pause, and pauses are priceless
because it allows us to go more into depth with something.
She continues, 'There is actually also something else that
I would like to talk about but I don't know where to start.
Can you help me?'

· · · · · · · · · · · · · ·

The question, 'How does telling me this make you feel?' can
also provide us with surprising new angles. Perhaps the person
you are trying to help has a fear of being judged, or a fear
of bursting into tears, or of coming across as strange, of not
getting in all the details of the story or of somehow betraying
the people she must include in the story that she is telling. She
may be in a dilemma over a specific maxim that forbids her
from speaking about people if they themselves are not present
to hear it.

Focusing both on the content of the words and on
everything else that is happening in the communication can be
particularly difficult if you are highly sensitive. You can easily
become overwhelmed by the multitude of information you are
given, all of which may initiate further aspects and ideas that
need to be taken into account. Once again, taking breaks will
come to play a significant role. Ask the person you are listening
to if you can take a moment's break so that you can absorb
and digest everything that you've heard so far. Remember that
the break not only benefits you but also functions as a kind
of breathing space or it can also be considered an interesting
challenge for the other person in terms of his or her personal
development. Mirroring, which is explained in Chapter 2 and
which entails repeating that which the other person has said,
may also be used to slow the pace of conversation. As you
repeat what you just have heard and possibly comment on any

other piece of information that you have received, for example via tone of voice or body language, you can use that space of time to absorb and digest the new information.

Drawing in the problem between the two of you

When listening to someone who has problems in a relationship it can be hard to judge who, in fact, has the problem. The narrator may tend to present the problem as though it really belongs to the other person involved and there is no way that you can hear the other side of the story. Moreover, getting long, detailed descriptions of what the other person did or didn't do can become tedious to listen to in the long run. So if, for example, a woman were to tell about how she struggles every time her colleague complains, you could ask, 'How would you feel if I were to start complaining about something?' You could possibly also do a little test where you add a few negative comments about the weather.

Talking about what is going on between the two of you, that is, turning the focus toward that which is going on right here and now between the 'I' and the 'you', is always more efficient than talking about the past. Here is another example:

Karin: I sometimes experience that other people look away when I talk to them. It must be because they don't like having to look at me. It often makes me think that there is something about my appearance that they don't like.

Helper: Did you notice that a moment ago I looked away as you were talking?

Karin: Yes, that's probably what made me think of it.

Helper: What about you might not be pleasant to look at?

Karin: I sometimes study myself in the mirror. I can't see what it could be but it might be something everyone else can see and that I can't.

Helper: Have you considered asking me what I see when I look at you?

Karin: I never dared to ask anyone…I worry about what they might say. Could you possibly tell me what you see, but just in small bits at a time so that it won't overwhelm me?

If it is possible to talk about a problem so that both of you can see it from two different angles, it can prove to be a very fruitful approach.

You can also intensify the effect of some of the other tools by introducing them into the exchange you are having with the person you are helping. If, for example, you want to train the other person in empathy, instead of asking, 'What do you think it's like to be your colleague?' you could, for example, ask, 'What do you think it's like being me right now?' or 'How do you think I'm feeling right now as I listen to you speak?' or 'How do you think hearing what you just said affects me?' However the person you are helping tends to think of others, whether in extremely enthusiastic terms or in extremely negative ones, the same tendency will apply in their relation to you. Perhaps the person you are helping thinks that you must be really very bored having to listen to them and can't wait for them to go home or perhaps they think that you are in awe and deeply impressed by what you are hearing. In both instances, the person you are helping will now have the opportunity to test his or her convictions and perhaps become more realistic with regard to their perception of how others are doing or how others perceive him or her.

In Chapter 1 I described how wishful fantasies may point the way for a person. If you ask the person whom you are helping what they want from you right there and then, the conversation will turn very intense. You could for example ask, 'Is there anything you can imagine me doing or saying that would make you feel really good?' If the person you are helping tends to crave acknowledgment from others this will also become apparent in relation to you. You two now have the opportunity to examine not only at close range but also from two different perspectives this exaggerated need for acknowledgment, a need which is most likely giving the person problems in his or her other relations.

There will, however, be situations where the method does not work, as, for example, if the problem does not emerge in relation to you or because the person is afraid of either revealing themselves to you or that you will feel criticised if he or she were to say anything but pleasing remarks.

Using the tools outside of the psychotherapeutic sphere

Personal development can first and foremost occur when a person becomes more aware of their considerations, emotions or experiences of what they like and don't like when they are talking with others. One way for you to study yourself would be for you to record yourself on video while speaking on the phone. When studying yourself afterwards, notice your body language and mimicry and try asking yourself some of the questions suggested at the beginning of this chapter, as for example, 'What considerations am I having as I select what I want to talk about?' 'Do I like what is going on?' 'Did the communication I just had on the phone with the other person bring me closer or further away from myself?' 'How do I want to be perceived by the other person?

For many people an exercise like that is a real eye-opener. You may become more aware of how you yourself appear to others and can use your knowledge about yourself to initiate a conversation with the other person about the relationship you have together. For example, if, when seeing yourself on video, you realise that you look more angry than you thought, you can bring up the topic by saying, 'I've thought about whether I come across as angry when we discuss your future possibilities. Do I seem angry to you? And how does that make you feel?'

It is better to reveal yourself as opposed to interrogating the other person. If you start by asking the other person a lot of questions, he or she may easily feel that they are being interrogated, which will only make them want to close off as opposed to opening up to you.

Focusing on what is happening between the helper and the person seeking help is also beneficial outside of the psychotherapeutic sphere. You can start out by asking whether the person would like to hear what you think, feel or how you experience the communication between the two of you. If the person says yes, he or she will get some very important information on how they come across to others. You can afterwards then challenge the person to express his or her feelings, thoughts and experiences while talking to you. Whenever we permit the conversation to deal with what's going on between you and me right here and now, we discover the significance or effect we have on one another. Most people really need to be on this level of consciousness much more than they normally are. That said, it does require a certain amount of courage to do so. Most people are not used to talking with one another in so direct a way.

If you are highly sensitive it may strike you as particularly intimidating to have to question someone so closely while having a dialogue with them, especially if you are not used to it. But if you practise doing it you will feel more comfortable about it and there are many benefits to be had from skipping over all the regular small talk and quickly getting to the heart of the matter, especially for highly sensitive helpers.

Summary

If instead of talking about something that has occurred at a different place in a different time, you start talking about what is happening here and now, the conversation will get very intense. It is seldom that we talk about our strengths or problems in such a direct way or exchange all the things we sense or experience as we talk together. However, if we do, there is a bigger chance that the conversation will be the kind that not only deepens the relationship but will also make a lasting impression.

The next chapter will deal with how you as a helper can help initiate growth when you meet people who are struggling with anxiety.

Chapter 8

How to Deal with Anxiety

Everyone is familiar with anxiety to a certain degree. The mildest type of anxiety is one which gives a person a slight sense of unrest. We are all familiar with situations where we are unable to relax, become restless or are on tenterhooks. Having a sense of fear or unrest may mean that we are approaching or are close to something that is extremely important to us. Most people experience a certain degree of unrest when speaking either about things they are struggling with or their most intense wishes and longings.

If the anxiety becomes too unpleasant for them, the person you are helping will most likely change the subject. If you are a psychotherapist you can choose to point out the fact that the topic of conversation is now changing and that the person may possibly be missing out on a chance for personal growth because he or she is avoiding really working through this very significant subject.

Outside of a psychotherapeutic sphere you must be more careful in such an instance, in which case it would be better to say that what you have just discussed seems significant and that you would like to talk more about it at a later point in time should the person feel so inclined.

If what you have been talking about with the person you are trying to help has proven to be difficult for them you can start talking more about their strengths by, for example, asking how he or she has managed to get through similar challenges earlier in their life. If you want to stick to their strengths you can pass lightly over their problems and enquire more into the successes they've experienced, as for example, 'What was it you did then that worked so well?'

Some people experience having an anxiety that is so strong that it in itself is a problem. If a person has experienced an actual panic attack he or she will typically be on guard for symptoms for fear of experiencing another one.

Panic anxiety

For people who have experienced having strong anxiety, what they sometimes fear the most is the anxiety itself more than anything else. That is why it is a matter of becoming friends with your anxiety. The more you know about anxiety, the less scary it becomes. If you are helping someone who is afraid of anxiety, you can start by getting them the necessary information they need. It is for example important to know how anxiety works on a physical level. Below is a description of it.

Humans are by nature equipped with an 'anxiety program'. If we sense that danger is near, our bodies prepare to either fight or flee in response if they don't freeze up completely like reptiles do in an attempt to trick the predator into thinking that they are dead.

Fight or flight

When our body prepares to take action, our heart rate and pulse will typically increase. We will often have the feeling that there is a heavy weight on our chest, feel dizzy or have other symptoms of discomfort. Our blood will start rushing to our bigger muscles, increasing our energy in our arms and legs so that we can run and fight more efficiently. However, that also means that blood is rushing away from our brain, making it harder for us to concentrate. It also rushes away from the stomach region, giving us butterflies in our stomach, queasiness, diarrhoea and we may even end up vomiting.

The anxiety 'process' was useful when people lived in caves and were hunted by enemy tribes and dangerous animals. However, in this day and age it merely gives people problems, for example, when you are going to give a lecture and suffer from queasiness moments before because your sense of anxiety is upsetting your stomach. But it is helpful to know that it is merely the anxiety process that has been initiated, that it will only last for a few minutes and that you are not about to get sick.

If you are sitting together with someone who is suffering from anxiety you can tell the person that the anxiety they are experiencing is not dangerous and that it will pass of itself. You can also help him or her to get into better contact with their body, which will decrease their sense of anxiety. Suggest that the person breathe all the way down to their fingers and toes or that they walk around a little and focus in on sensing their feet. The more contact they have with their body, the less anxiety they will feel.

Measure the anxiety and place it on a chair

By posing a question like, 'On a scale of one to ten how much anxiety do you feel right now?' you are helping the person to get out of their sense of being merged with their anxiety, thus allowing them instead to relate to it in an objective way. It is really a matter of being able to see your anxiety from the outside.

You can also get a chair and ask the person you are helping to imagine their anxiety is sitting on it. If he or she is able to enter into a dialogue with their anxiety it opens up the possibility for something new to occur. A question like, 'Anxiety, what do you want with me?' would be very relevant to ask. Perhaps the anxiety has a message that the person will be able to register by sitting down in its chair after posing the question. It is important to be open to whatever message the anxiety has. For example, have I put too many demands on myself for too long a time? Or am I changing and becoming a new and different person – a person with whom I still feel a bit estranged and not entirely at home with? Are there sides to me that have been dormant but that are now awakening? Søren Kierkegaard was of the belief that if you are leading a spiritually deprived life, the anxiety you are experiencing may, in fact, be a signal that your spirit is about to awaken.

Anxiety can seem diffuse and we are not always fully aware of what it is we fear. Kierkegaard (1981) distinguished between anxiety and fear. Fear usually arises in relation to something specific in which case it may be of extreme relevance to examine what the fear derives from.

Allow the person you are helping to work through their worst fears to completion

When we think of something that makes us scared we tend to quickly turn our thoughts toward something else that is more pleasant to think about. But in doing so we also tend to disrupt the anxiety we are experiencing at exactly the point where our worst fears have reached their peak. Perhaps we have an inner image of a catastrophe, an image that freezes and grudgingly sinks into the depths of our consciousness from which it always threatens to resurface.

Choosing to remain with the image instead of fleeing from it, and imagining your catastrophic situation to its completion can provide a sense of relief. Questions like, 'What are you most afraid of right now?' helps the person to embrace their anxiety and if things go really well the anxiety will disintegrate of itself once you get close enough to it. On the following pages you will find some examples.

Example 1:

> Per: There is going to be a round of lay-offs at my job next month. I'm really worried that I'm going to get fired.
>
> Helper: What would be the worst thing for you were you to get fired?
>
> Per: It could mean the start of my financial ruin.
>
> Helper: How do you imagine it coming to that?
>
> Per: If I am unable to find another job I will have to start receiving unemployment benefits, which will mean I won't be able to afford my house any longer. I'm also in doubt as to whether my marriage would be able to survive it.
>
> Helper: Let's say you have to go on unemployment benefits and have lost your house and wife. What would you do then?
>
> Per: Perhaps I'd end up living in a shelter with other homeless people.
>
> Helper: How long would you have to do that, do you think?
>
> Per: I just had another thought: If I lose both my house and wife I would no longer be bound by anything in particular and I've always wanted to travel and experience other cultures. I could perhaps do that as a development aid worker. (Per straightens up and his eyes light up.)
>
> Helper: So what good might come out of getting fired?
>
> Per: I still hope that I won't get fired, or that I can find another job if I do. But if the worst possible thing were to happen it might also open up new possibilities.

Example 2:

Ida: I am having difficulty concentrating right now. Sometimes I get a pain in my stomach and am afraid that it might be something serious.

Helper: What could it be if it were serious, do you think?

Ida: My father died of stomach cancer.

Helper: I can understand why you might be concerned about that. Let's say your fear turns out to be true, what would you be most afraid of?

Ida: It is not death that I fear most. I imagine that I would go somewhere that is peaceful. I'm not afraid of being in pain either because I saw how good they were at making sure that my father wasn't in pain. The worst thing would be my nine-year-old son. It would be so horrible for him.

Helper: How do you think he would react were you to die?

Ida: He would cry and be extremely unhappy. He would probably lie in his bed and cry. My husband would do everything to help him, but it would be impossible to console him.

Helper: For how many days do you think he'd lie in his bed crying like that?

Ida: After a few days he would probably get up and little by little start playing every now and then. But for a couple of weeks he'd probably be very sensitive and vulnerable and it wouldn't take much to upset him and he'd be back in bed again and inconsolable.

Helper: Imagine that it is six months since you passed away, how do you think he'd be doing then?

Ida: I think he'd be back to having a normal everyday life again but I also think he'd be a very serious type of boy.

Helper: What about five years later?

Ida: By that time I think he'd have worked through and gotten past it. He would probably be a silly and sometimes impossible teenager just like I was. But I think he'd be more mature for his age. I hope he'd be able to find a new mother figure. Phew! I can feel that I am able to take deep breaths again. I am actually able to deal with these thoughts. Life will go on no matter what happens to me.

When I help a person to examine the worst-possible scenario, I usually have the following questions in the back of my mind:

~ What is the worst possible thing that you imagine happening?

~ How long would it last?

~ What would you do?

~ Would you survive?

~ If the worst possible thing were to happen, will you be able to see something good coming out of it?

Oftentimes the person I am helping will answer the question themselves before I ever get a chance to ask them.

Whether you are a psychotherapist, professional helper or a friend, it is important before you get started asking questions about the worst-possible scenario, that you tell the person seeking help what he or she can get out of doing the exercise and ask whether the person would be willing to go on a journey that is often not very pleasant but will most likely take them to a more peaceful place.

Plan B

Examine whether the person you are helping has thought of a plan B. Just like there can be a sense of security in knowing where the lifeboats are when you're aboard a ship, it also comforting to have planned what you would do were plan A to fail.

Once when I was about to embark on a long journey, I was unable to fall asleep the night before for fear of something going wrong the following morning so that I'd miss my flight. I had set four alarm clocks so that it would be impossible for me not to hear them all. But what if my car wouldn't be able to start for some reason? I got up and checked the schedule for the nearest airport bus. Then I set the alarm clocks to ring a half an hour earlier so that I would have time to get up, see if the car would start and if it didn't still have time to catch a taxi to the airport bus. Once I laid out a plan I was better able to settle down.

It is also a good idea to have a plan B for what you can say to yourself or for what the person you are helping can say to him or herself if a project fails. Sometimes the fear one has of one's own judgment fills up a lot more space than one is aware of. Your courage to start a new project can therefore better grow if you have a set of soothing or acknowledging words you can say to yourself in case your endeavour doesn't go as planned. If, for example, you have invited someone to partake in a conversation about your relationship as it is here and now (see the previous chapter) and you don't get the result that you had hoped for you can plan in advance that instead of perceiving it solely as a fiasco you can say one of the following phrases below:

~ It was a good try.

~ You cannot make an omelette without breaking eggs.

~ Perhaps something good will still come of it in the long run.

~ Everyone has failed at something at some point in their lives; you can't luck out every time.

~ The experiences that I have gained by doing this are bound to serve me at a later time.

~ Some day when I am able to look back on this particular failure, I will laugh at it and tell my friends about it as a funny story.

~ It took a lot of courage for me to try taking that kind of a chance. Once I have recovered a little bit, I'll probably try taking another one.

This chapter is a very brief description of how you can confront anxiety. There is a lot of good literature out there about both the process and physiology of anxiety and the possible treatments thereof, some of which you can find in the bibliography list at the back of the book.

Summary

A very simple tool against anxiety is knowledge. People are afraid of the unknown. The more we know about the symptoms of anxiety and its process, the better we can tolerate it.

Getting to the very bottom of your worst fears about what might go wrong will for the most part result in the realisation that even if the worst possible thing were to happen, life would go on and there would be a way to move forward.

Making a plan B and perhaps also a plan C and D is like knowing where the exits are and how you can find your way to the lifeboats on a ship. Not only is it wise to know but it can also give you a sense of security knowing what to do if things should go wrong.

You are not necessarily highly sensitive even if you struggle with anxiety and not all highly sensitive people experience anxiety as a problem, but there is a big overlap. Highly sensitive people who were not given the support and caring they needed as children develop anxiety much easier than more robust people who have had a similar upbringing.

Since many highly sensitive people particularly enjoy and find a purpose in helping other highly sensitive people, I have written a chapter that examines what is important to know and remember when helping people who have this characteristic trait.

Chapter 9

IMPORTANT THINGS TO KNOW ABOUT HIGHLY SENSITIVE PEOPLE

Perhaps you are thinking that this chapter is somewhat superfluous to have in a book that is specifically intended for highly sensitive helpers who you would assume already know what it's like to have that characteristic. But highly sensitive people vary greatly. They don't all have all of the typical characteristics. Moreover, there are many highly sensitive people who would like to be cured of their sensitivity. If this chapter doesn't tell you anything you didn't already know, then enjoy getting reconfirmed in the things you intuitively knew.

You can also choose to read this chapter as a reminder of what you yourself may need, not only as a helper but as a person in general.

Some highly sensitive people also have a serious diagnosis, such as for example borderline personality disorder or schizophrenia. If you are not a trained psychotherapist with an extensive educational background and experience in the field, it is better that you recommend that the person seek professional help. Meanwhile, you can still continue to help them by using supportive tools like listening, mirroring and giving them the approval they need.

When it comes to everyday normal problems, a highly sensitive person is usually ideal for helping another highly sensitive person, regardless of whether the sensitive helper is a trained therapist, professional helper or just an ordinary caring human being. The similarities that highly sensitive people share in terms of, for example, their nervous systems and the ways that they function in life mean that they can mirror themselves in one another fairly accurately and with a high degree of empathic resonance.

Some people grow and develop best when they encounter resistance. Highly sensitive people are in more need of getting approval and being told that what they see and feel makes sense. They will be sure to ask themselves all the critical questions.

Below is a list of examples for what you need to be particularly aware of when the person you are helping is highly sensitive.

Highly sensitive people especially need acknowledgment and acceptance

Sometimes some not so sensitive therapists try to get sensitive people to become more extroverted. They tell them that they need to practise speaking more frankly and to stop considering their words beforehand and urge them to throw themselves into extroverted activities, explaining that it is wrong of them to always be worrying and anticipating trouble. They try to teach them to take things a little bit more as they come. Highly sensitive people are typically extremely cooperative and will, perhaps, continue to go to therapy for many years, putting the blame on themselves if it isn't working. And as they try to live up to the expectations of their therapist their self-esteem gets worse and worse.

It's actually intelligent to worry and consider your words before you speak when you are sensitive.

To be overwhelmed by too many impressions is such an unpleasant experience for the highly sensitive person that he or she will do whatever they have to in order to avoid it. Most highly sensitive people have discovered for themselves that the best thing is to be well-prepared both emotionally and mentally for the events that lie ahead of them. That way they will decrease the chances of their getting overly stimulated when the event happens. This strategy is often criticised by others as entailing too much worry and apprehension and so many sensitive people are ashamed of having such an uneasy psyche.

It's of course not good if you are constantly preoccupied with all the things that *might* happen in a moment. Some highly sensitive people need to learn to sometimes stop their train of thoughts and simply just enjoy being in the moment, which is possible to learn through various forms of disciplines such as, for example, meditation, yoga, mindfulness or other techniques where the focus is on the body and breath.

Imagining what might go wrong and always taking certain precautions is not a bad thing in itself. Most highly sensitive people are very good at it and it saves them from a lot of accidents and unpleasant situations. The power of imagination itself, which is often very vivid for them, may also be used to discover new possibilities and is very valuable in all sorts of creative work.

Love changes things

Most highly sensitive people have often been told, and usually also since childhood, that they ought to be different. Their surroundings wanted them to be less concerned, more cheerful and extroverted, faster in their reactions, more sociable, less sensitive and better to ignore the things that disturb their senses. They have also often compared themselves to others and attempted to live up to some rather extroverted values, thereby gradually growing further and further away from being the one they have the most talent to be.

To feel loved is to feel that you are seen and cared for exactly as the person you are. If you hardly know yourself and never dare to show what you know, there is a long way to go before you'll be seen by others. If you want to help a highly sensitive person to become stronger you should give them empathy, acknowledgment and acceptance as well as mirror them. If you say to the person that it would be better if he or she were stronger and more robust it will have the opposite effect: the sensitive person will feel unloved, become sad and feel even more vulnerable. As I mentioned in Chapter 2, 'the paradoxical law on change' is what is at play here. We do not change if others try to force us to; in fact, it will only make us feel insecure, and when you feel insecure, you lack the stamina to move or change yourself. On the other hand, if you experience that others see and accept you for exactly who you are, you gain strength and become stronger.

Shame and loyalty can get in the way of a flowing conversation

Highly sensitive people need to be encouraged to talk about who they are. I will typically ask them, 'Who are you? What do you want? What values do you have?' When they have told me something about themselves they need to be given some acknowledgment or mirrored with empathy as explained in Chapter 2. However, there may be various barriers when asking a highly sensitive person to speak frankly: many highly sensitive people are ashamed of themselves and the lives they lead. They are afraid of being judged were they to tell how little they themselves feel they get accomplished, or how much time they spend worrying about things. There can also be another reason why the highly sensitive person chooses not to speak openly: loyalty. Highly sensitive people are always very careful not to expose others.

If I ask a highly sensitive person to give me details about their parents regarding a specific situation and he or she becomes taciturn, I will typically ask how he or she is feeling as we are speaking about it. It usually becomes clear that the person I am helping is struggling with a sense of being disloyal. I assure them that I honour the obligation of confidentiality. In addition to that I'll ask them whether they don't think that their parents would have approved of their speaking honestly about themselves (and their childhoods) to me if they knew it would help them to talk about it. Saying that usually helps them to open up.

To tell one's story in a situation where one is met with acceptance and emotional resonance can be extremely fruitful for one's personal development. It may feel like being emotionally reconfirmed, which may also include one's entire existence.

As a lecturer and psychotherapist I find myself witnessing over and over again how highly sensitive people find the courage to be themselves, hold their heads high and find a more satisfying way to be in the world. However, there are particular problems that I hear over and over.

Problems that highly sensitive people typically have

Inappropriate surroundings

Highly sensitive people need a tranquil environment and a chance to retreat or shield themselves from social contact. If the one you are helping is not thriving it is a good idea to consider his or her surroundings and talk about his or her everyday life. There are many problems that can be solved simply by changing a person's surroundings, responsibility or working hours. Perhaps the person has been told that he or she has more problems than they actually do, and so it would be a great relief for them to discover that overstimulating and overly demanding surroundings are sometimes what create the problem in the first place.

Unstable self-support

It is important to examine the degree to which the highly sensitive person has a good and stable way of practising self-kindness because many of them don't. I will often ask them questions like, 'What did you say to yourself in that situation?' or 'What do you think of yourself?'

If it becomes apparent that their answers tend to turn into a series of self-reproaches and self-criticisms, then there is good reason to start practising a new way of behaving. If you ask the highly sensitive person what he or she would have said had it been a good friend who had come too late to a meeting and was sorry for it, they are usually extremely supportive of that person. But were the highly sensitive person do come too late to a meeting, they usually fill themselves with reproachful comments, such as, 'You should have planned your day better, pulled yourself together, taken into account that you might receive a phone call on the your way out the door...' Here is an example of a helpful conversation:

Sofie: I'm worried that I might make the wrong decision.

Helper: Well, let's say that you do. And later in time you realise that you should have made a different decision. What would you then say to yourself?

Sofie: I would say that I once again had managed to make a mistake and that I am not very good at making decisions.

Helper: Let's say that instead of you, your friend Katrine had made the exact same decision and gotten the same result, what would you have said to her then?

Sofie: Then I probably would have told her that she couldn't have known how things would turn out and that she undoubtedly had had the best of intentions when making the decision. Perhaps I'd also tell her that it was courageous of her to even make a decision.

Helper: Can you hear that you are actually speaking in an unloving way to yourself, even though you, in fact, know how to be supportive when it comes to other people?

Sofie: Yes.

What Sofie has to practise now is saying the same things to herself that she would have to her friend in the same situation. However, if she's been speaking in an unsupportive way to herself for many years, it may have become so ingrained in her that changing that pattern might not be so easy. But practice makes perfect. And once she's aware of the mechanism herself, she'll be very motivated to change it.

In my book, *Highly Sensitive People in an Insensitive World: How to Create a Happy Life* (2016b), I describe how you can practise writing caring and loving letters to yourself. Some can feel a difference once they've started focusing on the problem. Others need to write a caring and loving letter to themselves on a daily basis for some months before a new and steady pattern emerges.

Setting limits and accommodating your life in such a way that being in it is a pleasant experience is also a way of showing yourself love. The better you get at loving yourself, the more you will feel safe and at home in the world.

Without being in the habit of practising self-kindness on a steady basis, sensitive people tend to take all the blame for the negative things they experience, while giving others all the credit for the good things that happen to them.

Highly sensitive people sometimes take the
blame for things that really belong to others

Be aware of the fact that highly sensitive people tend to see all problems as being theirs. Here is an example.

Bodil tells me that she has difficulty expressing her anger in relation to her boss and that she wants to be better at expressing criticism and dissatisfaction. She doesn't like herself when she chooses to hold back instead of saying what she actually thinks.

Before I start suggesting ways that we can work through the problem, I present her to a small test that I usually give my clients. I ask her whether she has any other relationships in which she is unable to express dissatisfaction. If it turns out that she actually does, we start to examine with whom the problem arises within that particular relationship. Sometimes the problem can be narrowed down to only applying to people who react very negatively if they get criticised. For example, they may raise their voice or make a personal attack.

Seen in that light, it is actually clever to hold back when you are highly sensitive. Then it's actually a better idea to ask your trade union representative to talk with your boss or at least to bear witness to the conversation as opposed to forcing yourself to say something that you may intuitively know could possibly be taken the wrong way.

So the problem wasn't that Bodil is a coward as she initially deemed herself to be. The problem was that the boss was inflexible and unable to empathise with his employees when problems arose.

If you are helping a highly sensitive person, be aware of the fact that their tendency to take the blame for things which they really shouldn't may also become apparent in your relation to them. If your advice or exercises don't work for them, they may not tell you. On the contrary, they may even kindly thank you for your help and go home afterwards, blaming themselves for not being able to receive your help in the proper way.

When I suggest an exercise for the person to do at home, I try to eliminate any possibility there may be for them to take the blame if things don't work out by saying, for example, 'If you get home and find that you can't go through with the exercise it could be either because I have given you too difficult an exercise or my instructions haven't been clear enough. Also, not all the exercises work equally well on everybody, so if it doesn't work, just leave it alone for now.' Sensitive people are quick to put the blame on themselves and hesitate to put their own wishes and needs in the forefront.

Highly sensitive people sometimes forget to focus on themselves

When I speak with people who lack empathic skills, I help them by asking, 'How do you think it would be to be the other person in that situation?'

Sensitive people usually don't need to practise their empathic skills. They need to practise remembering to focus on themselves. So I ask them over and over, 'What did you feel at that moment? Did you like what was going on or didn't you? What do you wish should have happened?' It is not that they can't sense those things themselves, but they just often forget to focus on their own needs and feelings because they are so preoccupied with sensing and understanding the people in their immediate surroundings. They often start out talking about how it must have been to be the other person in a given situation while initially forgetting to notice their own feelings and signals.

In order for them to sense their own feelings again, highly sensitive people need to be surrounded by peace and tranquillity. As a helper, you can suggest that you sit together for a little while and try to encourage him or her to turn their focus inward.

Values and maxims

Sensitive people often have a stricter set of maxims compared to most people. So when you are helping a highly sensitive person it is a good idea to take an interest in their rules of conduct. Perhaps some of them could be eased up a little so that he or she has more capacity and energy to take action in his or her life. The ways in which you can work with maxims is described in Chapter 5.

If you have a strict set of rules it may be due to low self-esteem. It may also be a question of values. If you tend to follow more ethical rules than most people it may be because you think more in totalities and are good at seeing a situation from many different aspects. Sensitive people will often ask themselves the following question: 'If everyone acted like me, what would the world look like then?' They would hope to be able to answer that the world would then be a better place.

It is particularly in regard to two areas that I have noticed most sensitive people tend to take on a lot of responsibility and are actually pioneers within the fields, and those are in connection with preserving nature and issues on animal rights. For example, they will tell me that they can clearly sense how animals are doing and that they find an animal's life to be equally as valuable as a human life and almost can't bear to see an animal being treated in an unloving way. The same goes for the destruction of nature, which particularly tends to fill sensitive people with worry and pain. For them, nature is a source of joy and one that we should be deeply thankful for and it is for that reason that they feel guilty about ruining or polluting nature.

Values which are close to your heart and soul are ones that you, of course, shouldn't attempt to do away with, however easier life would be if you could. But being able to forgive yourself is important.

Forgiving yourself

Sensitive people mostly don't like to take part in the abuse of the earth's resources or polluting nature or causing others pain and grief. When they have to make a decision on a maxim they will typically ask themselves, 'Would there be an unfortunate consequence for people, animals or nature if I broke this rule or if I didn't?' It's almost always unfortunate for someone, if for no one else, then for one's self. No matter what we choose it will be unfortunate for someone or something. For example, my decision to sit down and write this book has meant that I am unable to be with my cancer-stricken mother, and that is unfortunate for her. Were I to choose to be with her instead, it would be unfortunate for me because my inspiration is so strong right now that my entire system would literally ache if I didn't follow it.

Many highly sensitive people feel so bad about making a decision that might be burdensome or unfortunate for others that they end up betraying themselves and their own source of life energy. They need to be reminded that though it is bad to do something that is unfortunate for someone else, the same most certainly holds true for themselves. They need to have concern for others and not least also themselves.

Many people need to be better at forgiving themselves. The more ethically responsible you want to be, the more complicated it gets. It is impossible to always do the right thing and you will often be in situations where you have to choose between a rock and a hard place. For example, I prefer to buy animal products that are ecological because that ensures, among other things, better animal welfare. But ecological sour cream is something I only can purchase in large quantities at my local supermarket, which means that I risk having to throw a lot of it out, something which I feel bad about. If I'm to feel bad about something or other every time I go out shopping then I've got to be good at forgiving myself when I break my own rules and appreciate myself for doing the best I can.

A maxim that completely forbids doing something that is burdensome to someone else makes it difficult to be in the world and requires such foresight and self-repression that it ruins joy and energy in life and that is too bad because we need both in order to create and achieve anything in this world.

When I'm out lecturing I'm often asked whether sensitivity can be cured. I will try to address that question in the following section.

What highly sensitive people can work on and what they must accept as conditional

Many highly sensitive people have had to listen to the numerous attempts of others to get them to come more out in the open so that they can get more hardened. But when they try, they get bad results or experiences. When highly sensitive people get overly stimulated, they tend to lose contact with themselves and may end up feeling somewhat helpless, which results in them making bad decisions and not functioning well socially.

It is not a good idea to try to harden yourself so that you can handle more impressions. For example, if I were to spend a considerable amount of time in various malls I'd just end up feeling ill and for no good reason.

The limits for how many stimulants you can take before it gets to be too much is, most probably, hereditary and cannot be altered by exposing yourself to many stimulants in the belief that you will eventually be able to learn to cope with them. You have to respect your own limits.

But there is something else that also effects how quickly you reach your limit. If you are scared, you will tend to scan your surroundings to ensure that there isn't any danger there and in that way end up taking in a lot of impressions at once. On the other hand, if you feel safe and look around in a relaxed way it will take longer for you to reach your limit. It is for that reason that it is very important that highly sensitive people feel safe and secure in life. A sense of safety is something you can find in your relationships. You can also get a sense of safety by getting to know yourself and feeling well-balanced. Knowing that you can always get support from at least one place, namely within yourself, may contribute to a sense of being more relaxed and present in life.

Highly sensitive people cannot harden themselves into being able to absorb more impressions, but they can delay the moment upon which they reach their limit in terms of over-stimulation by working on feeling more safe in life. With anxiety, however, it is different.

Anxiety is something highly sensitive people can work on

A number of highly sensitive people have anxiety over things like driving a car. When you're good at envisioning how wrong things can turn out, driving in traffic can seem very frightening. Some very sensitive people choose not to get a driver's licence. However, other problems arise from that as a result, because they end up becoming extremely dependent on others and things like getting home early from a party might prove difficult.

If you're worried about the responsibility entailed with driving a car, there are ways to alleviate that. If you defy your fear and drive in traffic anyway, you will find that it will feel less and less dangerous the more you do it. You will also soon discover that of the many things that can go wrong when driving in traffic, few things actually do. So, even though you may never become a completely relaxed driver, there is still something to be said for having the possibility to drive somewhere whenever one chooses.

Other highly sensitive people experience anxiety in connection with speaking in public. This is also something that needs to be looked at. For although their fear of standing out in public is great, the satisfaction they get from sharing their thoughts and seeing how much others get out of hearing them is just as great, if not greater.

It is important that more sensitive people fill the world with their thoughts and considerations. The American psychologist and researcher Elaine Aron believes that highly sensitive people are natural advisers. But that won't help anyone if they don't dare to stand out in public.

You can't harden yourself into being able to absorb more stimulants and impressions. But you can work with your anxiety and get used to it if you do whatever it is you are scared of enough times. So if a highly sensitive person has something he or she would like to share with the world, it is really a shame if they end up holding themselves back due to anxiety, because anxiety is something that gradually loses its grip on you the more you do whatever it is you fear.

However, there may be situations where the price you pay as a highly sensitive person for speaking out is too high. For example, if the other participants are not interested in the topic you are addressing and would clearly rather be speaking themselves and if several of them try to take over as a result, or if the highly sensitive person has to fight and raise his or her voice in order to even be heard, well, then the price is too high and the success rate too low.

If possible, the highly sensitive person needs to acquire the best possible conditions for his or her presentation. If it is possible to make an agreement with your boss that you initially be given the floor at a certain point, it would undoubtedly make things much easier. That way you, as a highly sensitive person, can concentrate on what it was you wanted to say and deal with whatever form of nervousness you may encounter.

When I started giving lectures I was very scared. My heart would pound and I would have breathing difficulties the first ten minutes of the lecture. I would prepare myself to deal with the anxiety attacks as well as I could. In the days leading up to the lecture I would envision becoming scared, maybe so scared that I wouldn't be able to say anything. I laid out a plan for myself as to what I would do should such a situation occur. Sometimes I would already get queasy and feverish the day before the lecture and I would even consider whether giving such a lecture really was worth all the discomfort I had to endure.

But I continued and now, 12 years later after my first lecture, I feel right at home giving lectures and I am very grateful that I stuck to it and continued. It is a really pleasant feeling to be able to take on a role in which you can fill the world with your words and your reality. As a highly sensitive person you often end up spending way too much time listening to others and identifying yourself with their world. Creating a platform in which you can speak uninterruptedly about the things you are passionate about provides a nice balance.

The reason why many highly sensitive people have a hard time speaking up may possibly have to do with the fact they have an extremely high set of standards for how interesting whatever it is they want to say must be before they feel that it is all right to take up other people's time with it. It may also be because they lack sufficient self-kindness within themselves. These are things that can be worked on.

Summary

There are various problems that highly sensitive people often have, some of which may include not having enough love for or being too critical of themselves and being in the habit of sensing other people's feelings better than their own. When highly sensitive people are given acceptance and empathy they end up feeling much better about themselves and that is usually enough for them to gain the strength they need to make the changes that are necessary for them to improve.

Highly sensitive people have a lower threshold when it comes to how many stimulants they can absorb compared to most people and that is something they have to learn to live with. Anxiety, however, is a different story, because it can, to a certain degree, be remedied.

The next chapter will deal with how you as a helper can take care of yourself. Whereas the tools that I have described up until now are meant to be used in supportive conversations, the following chapter will present tools that you can use to protect yourself against being too overwhelmed or overburdened.

Chapter 10

CHALLENGES FOR THE HIGHLY SENSITIVE HELPER

The sensitive nervous system

Your sensitive nervous system is responsible for the fact that you are able to sense the emotions and moods of other people so intensely that you practically experience those emotions as your own. That is an advantage, particularly when helping others, but it can also become burdensome.

You have probably often been told to not take things so seriously and instead just try to let the things you hear go through one ear and out the other without allowing it to affect you so much. The advice is usually given based on the idea that people tend to function similarly and what works for one person will also work for someone else. But if you are highly sensitive the things you experience will affect your psyche a lot more and you will need more time to digest and work through them.

In order to understand the difference between sensitive and more robust types of people it is important to be familiar with a study made by the American researcher Jerome Kagan (Kagan and Snidman 2004). Kagan tested 500 four-month-old babies and found that approximately every fifth baby reacted differently than the others. In the beginning he called these babies 'inhibited' children because they were more careful and cautious than the other children. Later he changed the description to 'high-reactive children'.

According to Kagan, a child who reacts strongly is one in whom a strong arousal may be registered when he or she is exposed to something new. The babies were exposed to, among other things, a balloon that burst, a colourful mobile which they were not familiar with and their mother looking at them while smiling as she normally would, the only difference being that she didn't say a word. Four out of five infants would stay calm and relaxed but every fifth would react and cry and wave their arms.

Kagan later gathered the children again when they were two, four, seven and eleven years old and found each time that the children who reacted strongly as babies also stood out later in life by reacting strongly to new impressions.

The term highly reactive is not to be confused with being outwardly reacting, which is something entirely different. What I am referring to here is solely an *inner* reaction or movement. While babies who react strongly scream more and gesticulate when something new happens in their surroundings, once they get older the strong internal reactions that these children typically have may not be visible. The only thing you may be able to see is that the child tends to hide behind his mother or father when encountering strangers. In other words, the babies who screamed and gesticulated were not the ones who later became noisy teenagers. On the contrary, they will most likely develop into quiet and reserved types who reflect more over life than do their peers.

The American psychologist and researcher Elaine Aron thinks that the children in Kagan's research who are 'high reactives' are in reality highly sensitive children and Kagan's research is important in her description of highly sensitive people (Aron 1997, 2010).

She has since done research in the reactions of highly sensitive adults when they are introduced to various impressions by placing them in a brain scanner and her research results have been published in the international scientific journal *Brain and Behavior* (Acevedo *et al.* 2014).

Eighteen people were scanned as they looked at pictures of faces that were either happy or sad. There were both pictures of strangers and of the person's romantic partner.

It became apparent that the areas of the brain associated with empathy including the mirror neuron system were considerably more active in highly sensitive people than with the other testees. Activity was at its highest in highly sensitive people when they saw a picture of their romantic partner smiling. The emotions of other people – positive as well as negative – created more internal arousal in highly sensitive participants than in others.

Many highly sensitive helpers blame themselves for being unable to follow the advice of others when they tell them not to let the things they hear affect them so deeply. But you cannot blame yourself for something which you have no control over. You yourself have not chosen to have strong reactions to things and you cannot just choose to dismiss having them even though it would make life much easier if you could. What you *can* do, and what is important that you do, is take really good care of yourself.

Protecting yourself against becoming overwhelmed by the other person's narrative or emotional expression

If you have a maxim that demands that you are 100 per cent available to the person you are helping you may tend to maintain very open body language as well as an open direct gaze, which you probably have difficulty averting without feeling guilty. We register the other person's emotional state with our entire sensory apparatus.

A certain distance needs to be created in order for us not to get too overwhelmed. If the other person's reality is straining for you, I suggest that you experiment with creating more distance between the two of you and that your body posture remain only partially open, which will allow you to focus some of your attention on also sensing your own feelings. Sitting across from the person you are listening to may not be ideal for you. Try sitting with your side to them, or just slightly skewed. That way you will feel more at liberty to, among other things, look in a different direction if you need to.

When we look away or look down, we are signalling that our focus has turned inward. Highly sensitive people need to do that more often than others and are therefore oftentimes the first ones to avert their eyes. Eighty per cent of the impressions we get come through the eyes and when there is an intense form of eye contact there will undoubtedly also flow an intense stream of information. When you can sense that you are approaching the limit for how much information you can absorb it is crucial that you take that limit seriously if you want to preserve your own energy. Allow yourself to avert your eyes for a moment when you feel the need to and practise withstanding your sense of guilt if the other person seems to react in frustration. If the person doesn't feel like talking to you when you are looking down he or she will have to take a break until you are ready again. Good communication consists of catching, holding and letting go of eye contact. The more you allow yourself to let go and return, the better you will be able to be present in your connection with the other person and keep up your energy.

As a highly sensitive person you are typically not good at focusing your attention on more places than one. At worst, you will become so absorbed by what you are listening to that you may completely lose contact with yourself. Practise shifting the focus back and forth during the conversation. Switch between looking at the person you are helping, listening to their words and sensing his or her feelings and moods, and then turn your gaze away and sense your own feelings.

You both need to be in your consciousness if the contact is to be good.

Many sensitive people have the need to leave the room every once in a while in order to fully sense their own feelings. Sometimes they even need to leave the building before they again are ready to be more present in the connection.

Do as much as you can and take breaks

Sometimes highly sensitive people don't fully grasp their own need for breaks. But when you consider the strong inner reactions they get from impressions and how often they bear other people's pain, having to take breaks makes good sense. Don't bother comparing yourself to what others are capable of. Just do what you can and know that the effect of the good that you are doing is most likely much greater than you yourself realise.

Highly sensitive people can offer a connection and a form of presence that is of a very high quality. Many of them are experts in providing a kind of empathic resonance that confirms the feelings of others and that can have a healing effect on them. They just can't do it for many hours at a time.

You can take your breaks with a clear conscience. No one has any claim on receiving more from you than you are capable of offering them. Everyone is responsible for his own life.

To be a midwife for new insights or just being helpful

It is better to teach a hungry man how to fish than to give him fish. And it is better to teach the person you are helping to sow his or her own seeds and bake his or her own bread as opposed to just receiving everything from you.

Continuing to serve and compensate instead of helping the other person start to practise bearing their own burdens is a pitfall that highly sensitive people in particular tend to succumb to. Sometimes they are so good at filling other people's gaps that while everyone around them may seem to be doing well in a number of ways, sensitive people may find themselves becoming increasingly tired and lacking energy, which may result in others feeling sorry for them.

Giving empathy can be very important. However, highly sensitive helpers can sometimes become so empathic that they, inadvertently, end up supporting and encouraging behaviour in others that really ought to be changed. Below are some examples.

If you give an alcoholic some beer he will consider you to be helpful and will thank you for it. If you instead offer him a sandwich and talk with him about his problem he will probably respond with anger, but in the long run you may have contributed to his ability to overcome his substance abuse. And if you have a colleague who typically blames others for her problems and you confirm her in her conviction that her husband ought to change, she will consider you to be kind and helpful. If you were to ask instead, 'How do you think he sees the problem?' you are helping her to see the issue from a different angle, which will allow for a lot more growth, even if she seems less enthusiastic about it at first.

Another example might be a woman who enthusiastically tells about some decisions that she made the results of which will be beneficial in the short term but which you clearly see will not be advantageous either for her or others in the long term. You will in all probability feel a need to support her in her decisions and share in her joy as you feel that she wants you to. At the same time you will probably sense a certain reluctance on your part to confront her with the unfavourable consequences of her decisions.

I myself have needed to work at pointing out inappropriate patterns as opposed to just being helpful. If you don't like being confronted with anger, it can be tempting to just give in to the things others ask for as opposed to teaching them something new and providing them with something from which they can grow. This is an aspect which most highly sensitive people ought to be aware of. The price you pay for being more helpful than contributing to a person's personal growth is having to listen to them sing the same old tune over and over.

The reason why highly sensitive people are easy prey in serving other people's negative patterns is their reluctance to be confronted with the dissatisfaction of others. And when they don't just cast aside the burdens of others and give them a course in how to take care of themselves, it is often because they tend to easily feel responsible for the pain others are experiencing. Studies show that highly sensitive children tend to have a stronger sense of guilt than others when they have done something that they regret that they did (developmental psychologist and researcher Grazyna Kochanska, in Kochanska and Thompson 1998). This increased tendency to take on the blame can easily be abused by others who may try to cross the highly sensitive person's boundaries. Luckily it is possible for highly sensitive people to become less susceptible to having feelings of guilt.

Practise withstanding your feelings of guilt

Feeling guilty is often the same as being afraid of being punished by others or experiencing their anger. If Cecilie, whom I described in the introduction, instead of continuing to listen to her husband's endless complaints, were to say to him that she from now on will only listen to him speak of his dissatisfaction for one hour a week until he has found a solution to his problem he will probably feel bad for a period of time and in all likelihood get angry over her rejection. The 'apprenticeship test' for Cecilie is for her to actually announce it to him. The final test would be for her to withstand her subsequent sense of guilt so that she can hold on to her decision.

This is an area where highly sensitive people often need to practise in 'holding out' or withstanding so that they can better accept their own feelings of guilt and shame.

If you absolutely cannot stand feeling guilty about something you are most likely doing everything you can to fulfil everyone else's expectations. Many highly sensitive people live that way and allow themselves to be made use of in other people's 'dance of avoidance'.

You can practise enduring a sense of guilt as opposed to just right away trying to do everything possible to make it go away. Because when you give into the wishes of others you will find that although you may sometimes make people happy in the short term, in the long term they will not benefit from it and neither will your friendship with them.

The ability to endure others becoming disappointed in us from time to time can give us a lot of freedom. Registered psychotherapist and theologist Bent Falk (2010) calls guilt feelings a form of existential added tax value. It is a price which we sometimes have to pay in order to be ourselves and allow ourselves to be steered from within as opposed to being steered by others.

When others get disappointed with you it is sometimes because you have sensed within, felt your own feelings, found your own truth, which you have chosen to act upon as opposed to following the directions of others.

It may be helpful to Cecilie if she were to remind herself that even though she can see that Hans is suffering as a consequence of her rejection, what she has chosen to do is by far the best decision in the long term both for herself and for their relationship. And not least for Hans, even though he will most likely be unable to see that it is just now.

If you think it is your responsibility alone you will most likely end up worn out and exhausted.

Tools against taking too much responsibility

Highly sensitive people have a tendency to take too much responsibility. It is therefore very important that if you help others you also make sure that you don't take too much responsibility for something that you don't really have control over. You cannot be responsible for something you do not control. And if you take responsibility for someone else whose behaviour you can't control, you will end up working too much and thereby risk excessively consuming your very own energy without anyone really benefiting from it in the end.

When highly sensitive people see others in distress they often feel that they ought to come to the rescue and alleviate the problem like an emergency ambulance. And it's not always the wrong thing to do. But there are other things that could work just as well and sometimes even better in the long run.

Very sensitive people often tend to immediately shift their focus on and invest their energy into feelings of guilt when the people around them are doing badly and they have been unable to help them. If you are one of those people, the description below of how you can let go of some of that bound-up energy may be helpful to you.

Consider what you say to yourself if the people around you are doing badly. Let's say it's your sister. You may say the following, 'Oh no, now she's doing badly again. I've tried to help but apparently it isn't helping. I wonder what it is I've done wrong?'

In such a case, I recommend that you replace that sentence with one of the following:

~   What competences does my sister need to learn in order for her to feel better?

~   What can she learn from this?

If you are in the habit of saying to your sister, 'Is there anything I can do to alleviate your pain?' then try replacing it with one of the following sentences:

~ What can you do to feel better?

~ What are you *willing* to do to feel better?

~ Considering the many challenges you've experienced in your life, there is no doubt in my mind that you can find the right solution for this.

Remind yourself that challenge can be a great opportunity for growth. People who get many scars often develop more personal potential for growth and a more interesting personality than people who have always had things go their way. So if you haven't managed to protect your loved ones from getting scars, you can comfort yourself with the thought of all the personal growth they have the chance to experience as a result.

Some highly sensitive people throw everything overboard, including their own needs, if someone in their vicinity bursts into tears. But there is another possibility, and that is saying the following: 'Just have a good cry, you probably need it.'

However, there is nothing that is ever the right way of doing something. Giving someone bread when they are hungry may be experienced as love. And sometimes that is exactly what people need in order to get the necessary energy to change their situation. If you shower your friend with love when you discover that he or she is suffering, that may be the exact thing they need in order to get through the crisis wholly intact. Love is the strongest curative element we know.

But if using this strategy means that you are expected to constantly come rushing at all odd times of the day, it is better to hold back so that your friend can learn to plant their own seeds and harvest their own crop.

Helping others in hope of receiving something in return

If the person you are with is so depleted of energy that he or she is unable to give you what you want or need, it is a good idea to try helping them. Highly sensitive children in energy-depleted families grow up to be very accommodating and helpful. They do what they can to help their family's energy grow.

If your partner is experiencing a crisis it is a good idea to hold back a little on your own wishes and needs and provide your partner with help and the space he or she needs to work through his or her own crisis so that they may gain energy to partake in a mutual relationship in which both parties give and take on an equal basis.

The problem is that some highly sensitive people end up playing a certain role subconsciously. They continue to help and hold themselves back and are sometimes not even aware of just how much they subconsciously wish that it will someday be their turn to receive help.

If you discover that you are helping others while at the same time carrying such expectations it is a good idea to be entirely realistic. Do you have substantial enough reason to believe that the person you are helping will some day feel well enough to partake in a relationship with you on a more equal footing? Try asking someone who knows both you and the other person. It can be hard to evaluate one's own close relationships.

If you do not have substantial enough reason to hope for change it is a good idea to let your hope go. If it is important for you to be in a relationship that is more mutual, you might consider finding a different one where the exchange between giving and receiving is shared more equally. You can also stay in the relationship and continue to help and enjoy the sense of purpose and happiness you can get from helping another person. If you offer to help because it gives you joy as opposed to expecting something in return, you will be much less frustrated in the relationship in the long run.

Many people waste the possibilities they get in their lives because they cling to certain expectations that are not realistic and are therefore unable to accurately evaluate the situations they face and are thus unable to take appropriate action based on reality. If you have a hard time facing reality you may get a lot out of reading my book *Come Closer: On love and self-protection* (Sand 2017).

Find the courage to stand your ground

I believe it is every person's task to be true to themselves and dare to sense their own feelings and stand their ground in the midst of the great human diversity that we carry within each of us. The more you are able to be self-contained, the more your contribution to the world will become apparent, thereby making you a better helper.

Our inner lives have different forms of expression at different times. In the role of the helper it is sometimes expressed in joy, as in, 'Good thing I'm not the one experiencing that.' That is an entirely legitimate feeling. You could also call it being grateful. That is one of the benefits of helping others, constantly being reminded of the problems one *doesn't* have. At other times we will experience a sense of fatigue and a desire to ask the person we are helping to pull themselves together. Again, it is entirely legitimate to grow tired and not feel like continuing any longer.

If you are insecure about your own inner reality or are ashamed of it, it may be tempting to allow the other person's reality to take up all your attention. I am often asked about what you can do to avoid being too affected by the emotions and moods of other people. Being familiar with your own feelings and senses and having a strong sense of self-support makes it easier to maintain contact with yourself while at the same time maintaining a sense of connection with others. And the stronger the contact you have with your own core the less likely it is that you will become overwhelmed by others when they express themselves.

Taking care of yourself

It is important that there is also someone there to listen to you. If you yourself spend a lot of time listening to others tell about their struggles, then you especially need to have a place you can go to with your own struggles and with the thoughts and concerns that naturally arise when others confide in you.

Perhaps you are a professional helper and are receiving the supervision you need through your work place. If you are helping friends and acquaintances and don't have a work place that can provide you with support you will have to find it yourself. You could, for example, go regularly to a psychotherapist or psychologist. You can also find a group where you listen to and provide each other with mutual support. It is important that you get a chance to share your experiences as a helper as well as your considerations as to how you can best help not only the other person but also yourself.

If you are in a process where others help you reflect on yourself as a helper, your talents and skills for helping will undoubtedly be strengthened and enhanced as a result, making you better equipped and faster at determining when you should intervene in a situation and when you should hold back. You will find your success rate increasing, which makes it not only easier but also a lot more fun to be a helper.

Of all the people you are helping, the first person to come at the top of your list should be you. When flying in a plane we are always instructed to put on our own oxygen mask before helping others to do the same. As a highly sensitive person one of the most important tasks is making sure that you yourself live in an environment that is healthy and that you can thrive in and don't become too overly stimulated. And if that is all that you are capable of right now, that is fine too.

Remember to also use your empathic talents on yourself. Practise sensing your own needs just as you sense those of others. Taking good care of yourself is, and always should be, your first priority. Otherwise you risk becoming a problem for others in the long run because you may end up functioning badly as a result or even becoming sick.

Once you find the right balance and give that which you are capable of offering and learn to feel good about it, even if it just means helping someone out for an hour a year, you will experience a wonderful feeling of joy and sense of purpose once you notice that you are able to help others thrive.

Summary

The big problem for highly sensitive people is that they typically grow tired and forget to use their talent for helping others on themselves. They typically become very preoccupied with the people they are helping and overlook the times when they themselves grow tired and find themselves in need of something that will give them back their energy.

Highly sensitive people can provide more space for themselves if they are better able to accept and accommodate their own feelings of guilt and, if necessary, are able to limit their sense of over-responsibility.

The World Needs Helpful Souls

If you are a sensitive person you most likely have the need to act in the world in a certain way that makes sense to you and that goes beyond fulfilling your own needs. Some sensitive people express themselves through creativity or music and in that way create joy and depth in the world. Others help solve practical problems and still others use the art of helping dialogues.

I hope that after having read this book you have gotten some ideas and the courage to practise and enhance your competencies for helping others so that you can get the best out of the resources you have at hand. It is important that you aren't thriftless with your valuable ability because you want to help each and every person that you happen to meet where some of them might be better off learning to help themselves.

It is my hope that by using the tools in this book you will be better able to work with and practise providing precisely the kind of help that is needed at the exact right moment. I also hope that you have become more aware of the importance of using your empathic skills on yourself as well and of listening to what your body and soul need so your energy can last as long as possible. The world needs your help.

Know that you are not alone. There are helpful souls and other good resources all over the world and there is no need for you to be nor to carry the entire ocean. Just a single drop.

Enjoy your work…

WRITE A FAREWELL LETTER

Let the questions inspire you or write something entirely different. As long as it comes from the heart.

~ What are the pleasant things that you have lost?

~ What do you want to say thank you for?

~ What is unpleasant in the relationship? What it is that you wish to free yourself of?

~ What do you wish you had gotten from the person?

~ What did you give in the relationship? (For example, 'I think you became happy when I…' or, 'I think your pain receded when I…')

~ What would you have liked to have given more of?

~ How do you wish that your relationship had been?

~ What do you wish you could have done together with the person today?

~ What have you missed in the relationship?

~ What do you wish for the person?

THANKS TO...

Registered psychotherapist and theologist Bent Falk whose wise and intelligent words I have been listening to with pleasure in various contexts for many years.

Thanks to all of you who over the years have shown me the confidence to share your thoughts and emotions – either when providing pastoral care, in my work as a therapist, when giving lectures or elsewhere. I am especially grateful to those of you who have given your permission for me to use your stories in this book.

Also thank you to those of you who have read through the manuscript of this book and provided me with feedback. Without that sparring which I have shared with you, the book would not have been nearly as precise in its articulation and expression. I would especially like to mention the names: Ellen Boelt, Margith Christiansen, Martin Håstrup, Janet Cecilie Ligaard, Kirstine Sand and Lykke Strunk. You have in each your own way left your mark on this book.

BIBLIOGRAPHY

Acevedo, B.P., Aron, E.N., Aron, A., Sangster, M.-D., Collins, N. and Brown, L.L. (2014) 'The highly sensitive brain: an fMRI study of sensory processing sensitivity and response to others' emotions.' *Brain and Behavior*, Open Access. Available at http://hsperson.com/pdf/The_highly_sensitive_brain_%20an_fMRI_study.pdf, accessed on 17 January 2017.

Aron, Elaine (1997) *The Highly Sensitive Person*. New York: Broadway Books.

Aron, Elaine (2001) *The Highly Sensitive Person in Love: Understanding and Managing Relationships When The World Overwhelms You.* New York: Broadway Books.

Aron, Elaine (2010) *Psychotherapy and the Highly Sensitive Person: Improving Outcomes for That Minority of People Who Are the Majority of Clients.* New York: Routledge.

Boyce, W.T., Chesny, M., Alkon, A., Tschann, J.M. *et al.* (1995) 'Psychobiologic reactivity to stress and childhood respiratory illness: results of two prospective studies.' *Psychosomatic Medicine 57*, 411–422.

Buber, Martin (2010) *I and Thou*. Eastford, CT: Martino Fine Books.

Cain, Susan (2013) *Quiet – The Power of Introverts in a World That Can't Stop Talking.* London: Penguin.

Davidsen-Nielsen, Marianne and Leick, Nini (1991) *Healing Pain: Attachment, Loss, and Grief Therapy.* New York: Routledge.

Falk, B. (2010) *At være der, hvor du er.* København: Nyt Nordisk Forlag.

Jaeger, Barrie (2004) *Making Work Work for the Highly Sensitive Person.* New York: McGraw-Hill Books.

Jung, C.G. (1948) *Die Beziehungen der Psychotherapie zur Seelsorge.* Zürich: Rascher Verlag.

Jung, C.G. (1955) *Vesuch Einer Darstellung Der Psychoanalytischen Theorie.* Zürich: Rascher & Cie AG.

Jung, C.G. (1976) *Psychological Types.* Princeton, NJ: Princeton University Press.

Kagan, Jerome and Snidman, Nancy (2004) *The Long Shadow of Temperament.* Cambridge, MA: Belknap Press, Harvard University Press.

Kierkegaard, Søren (1981) *The Concept of Anxiety.* Princeton, NJ: Princeton University Press.

Kierkegaard, Søren (1998*) The Point of View for My Work as an Author.* Edited and translated by Howard V. Hong and Edna H. Hong. Princeton, NJ: Princeton University Press.

Kochanska, G. and Thompson, R.A. (1998) 'The Emergence and Development of Conscience in Toddlerhood and Early Childhood.' In J. E. Grusec and L. Kuczynski (eds) *Handbook and Parenting and the Transmission of Values.* New York: Wiley.

Laney, Marti Olsen (2002) *The Introvert Advantage: How to Thrive in an Extrovert World.* New York: Workman Publishing Company.

O'Toole, Donna (1988) *Aarvy Aardvark Finds Hope.* Burnsville, NC: Compassion Press.

Rosenberg, Marshall B. (2003) *Non-violent Communication: A Language of Life.* Encinitas, CA: PuddleDancer Press.

Sand, Ilse (2016a) *The Emotional Compass: How to Think Better about Your Feelings.* London: Jessica Kingsley Publishers.

Sand, Ilse (2016b) *Highly Sensitive People in an Insensitive World: How to Create a Happy Life.* London: Jessica Kingsley Publishers.

Sand, Ilse (2017) *Come Closer: On Love and Self-Protection.* London: Jessica Kingsley Publishers.

Yalom, Irvin D. (1980) *Existential Psychotherapy.* New York: Basic Books.